Lecture Notes in Computer Science   14563

Founding Editors

Gerhard Goos

Juris Hartmanis

Editorial Board Members

The series Lecture Notes in Computer Science (LNCS), including its subseries Lecture Notes in Artificial Intelligence (LNAI) and Lecture Notes in Bioinformatics (LNBI), has established itself as a medium for the publication of new developments in computer science and information technology research, teaching, and education.

LNCS enjoys close cooperation with the computer science R & D community, the series counts many renowned academics among its volume editors and paper authors, and collaborates with prestigious societies. Its mission is to serve this international community by providing an invaluable service, mainly focused on the publication of conference and workshop proceedings and postproceedings. LNCS commenced publication in 1973.

Bin Sheng · Hao Chen · Tien Yin Wong
Editors

Myopic Maculopathy Analysis

MICCAI Challenge MMAC 2023
Held in Conjunction with MICCAI 2023
Virtual Event, October 8–12, 2023
Proceedings

Springer

Editors
Bin Sheng 🄳
Shanghai Jiao Tong University
Shanghai, China

Hao Chen
The Hong Kong University of Science
and Technology
Hong Kong, China

Tien Yin Wong
Tsinghua University
Beijing, China

ISSN 0302-9743   ISSN 1611-3349 (electronic)
Lecture Notes in Computer Science
ISBN 978-3-031-54856-7   ISBN 978-3-031-54857-4 (eBook)
https://doi.org/10.1007/978-3-031-54857-4

Preface

Myopic Maculopathy (MM) can lead to severe visual impairment and even blindness. Timely intervention and treatment are key to preventing its further progression. The integration of artificial intelligence (AI) algorithms into MM diagnosis is a major advancement in ophthalmology. These AI-driven systems could reduce the workload of ophthalmologists by improving diagnostic efficiency and accuracy. However, the development of deep learning algorithms for this purpose is hampered by the difficulty of obtaining accurately labeled datasets. Labeling for MM requires specialized knowledge and is a time-consuming process, yet it is crucial for training effective deep learning models. Moreover, the scarcity of publicly available datasets for MM diagnosis hampers the ability to benchmark and evaluate the performance of these AI systems. Therefore, addressing these challenges is essential for leveraging the potential of AI in improving the diagnosis and management of MM, ultimately leading to improved patient care and outcomes in the field of ophthalmology.

To address this limitation, we organized the Myopic Maculopathy Analysis Challenge (MMAC 2023), which was a part of the 26th International Conference on Medical Image Computing and Computer Assisted Intervention (MICCAI 2023). The challenge consisted of three clinically relevant subtasks: classification of myopic maculopathy (Task 1), segmentation of myopic maculopathy plus lesions (Task 2), and prediction of spherical equivalent (Task 3). For Task 1, the dataset consisted of 1143 training images, 248 validation images, and 915 testing images. In Task 2, the dataset was divided for the segmentation of lacquer cracks (LC) with 63 training images, 12 validation images, and 64 testing images; for choroidal neovascularization (CNV) with 32 training images, 7 validation images, and 22 testing images; and for Fuchs spots (FS) with 54 training images, 13 validation images, and 45 testing images. For Task 3, the dataset consisted of 992 training images, 205 validation images, and 806 testing images. The datasets for these tasks were collected from two data centers. Metadata information was provided for each image, including age, sex, height, and weight. Some of the images had incomplete metadata.

The submission and automated evaluation for the challenge were carried out using the Codalab platform (codalab.lisn.upsaclay.fr). Participants were granted access to the dataset after registering on the platform and agreeing to the challenge rules through a signed consent form. Furthermore, participants were able to access detailed information about the challenge, including rules, news updates, timelines, and their rankings, on the official challenge website. Upon completion of the challenge, each participating team was required to submit a comprehensive paper detailing their results and methodology. This submission was expected to cover various aspects such as data preprocessing, data augmentation, model architecture, optimization strategies, and post-processing techniques. For teams participating in multiple tasks, there was the option to submit either individual papers for each task or a single paper covering all the methods in different tasks. In the end, we received eleven papers from the participant teams, presenting diverse methodologies: seven for the first task, four for the second, and four for the third. These teams were considered for the final official ranking. Some teams were also invited to present their work at a half-day satellite event during MICCAI 2023 to share their contributions and findings.

This proceeding contains eleven papers, each of which explores a range of state-of-the-art deep learning methods developed for the various tasks presented in the challenge. Each paper underwent a single-blind peer review process, involving a minimum of three reviewers. This review focused on assessing the novelty, writing, format, and overall quality of the work.

We would like to express our sincere gratitude to all participants of MMAC 2023, challenge committee members, reviewers, and MICCAI organizers. Their efforts and invaluable contributions were instrumental in the successful organization of this challenge.

January 2024   Bin Sheng
                                                            Hao Chen
                                                      Tien Yin Wong

Organization

General Chairs

Bin Sheng — Shanghai Jiao Tong University, China
Hao Chen — The Hong Kong University of Science and Technology, Hong Kong, China
Tien Yin Wong — Tsinghua University, China

Program Committee

Yih-Chung Tham — Singapore Eye Research Institute, Singapore National Eye Centre, Singapore
Ching-Yu Cheng — Singapore Eye Research Institute, Singapore National Eye Centre, Singapore
Marcus Ang — Singapore Eye Research Institute, Singapore National Eye Centre, Singapore
Carol Y. Cheung — The Chinese University of Hong Kong, Hong Kong, China
Qiang Wu — Shanghai Jiao Tong University Affiliated Sixth People's Hospital, China
Rongping Dai — Peking Union Medical College Hospital, China
Xinyuan Zhang — Beijing Tongren Hospital, China
Jie Shen — Shanghai Jiao Tong University Affiliated Sixth People's Hospital, China
Feng Lu — Huazhong University of Science and Technology, China
Mingang Chen — Shanghai Development Center of Computer Software Technology, China
Xiaokang Yang — Shanghai Jiao Tong University, China
Yaohui Jin — Shanghai Jiao Tong University, China
Haitao Song — Shanghai Jiao Tong University, China
Yang Wen — Shenzhen University, China
Yinfeng Zheng — Zhongshan Ophthalmic Center, Sun Yat-sen University, China
Huating Li — Shanghai Jiao Tong University Affiliated Sixth People's Hospital, China
Pheng-Ann Heng — The Chinese University of Hong Kong, Hong Kong, China

Daniel Ting	Singapore Eye Research Institute, Singapore National Eye Centre, Singapore
Gavin Siew Wei Tan	Singapore Eye Research Institute, Singapore National Eye Centre, Singapore
Xiangning Wang	Shanghai Jiao Tong University Affiliated Sixth People's Hospital, China
Bo Qian	Shanghai Jiao Tong University, China
Tingyao Li	Shanghai Jiao Tong University, China
Gengyou Huang	Shanghai Jiao Tong University, China
Zhengrui Guo	The Hong Kong University of Science and Technology, Hong Kong, China
Tingli Chen	Huadong Sanatorium, China
Jia Shu	Shanghai Jiao Tong University, China
Yan Zhou	Peking Union Medical College Hospital, China

Data and Technical Contributors

Xiuyuan Chen	Shanghai Jiao Tong University, China
Shangmin Huang	Shanghai Jiao Tong University, China
Ruixue Zhang	Zaozhuang University, China

Contents

Automated Detection of Myopic Maculopathy in MMAC 2023:
Achievements in Classification, Segmentation, and Spherical Equivalent
Prediction 1
    Yihao Li, Philippe Zhang, Yubo Tan, Jing Zhang, Zhihan Wang,
    Weili Jiang, Pierre-Henri Conze, Mathieu Lamard, Gwenolé Quellec,
    and Mostafa El Habib Daho

Swin-MMC: Swin-Based Model for Myopic Maculopathy Classification
in Fundus Images 18
    Li Lu, Xuhao Pan, Panji Jin, and Ye Ding

Towards Label-Efficient Deep Learning for Myopic Maculopathy
Classification 31
    Junlin Hou, Jilan Xu, Fan Xiao, Bo Zhang, Yiqian Xu, Yuejie Zhang,
    Haidong Zou, and Rui Feng

Ensemble Deep Learning Approaches for Myopic Maculopathy Plus
Lesions Segmentation 46
    Fan Xiao, Junlin Hou, Jilan Xu, Yiqian Xu, Bo Zhang, Yuejie Zhang,
    Haidong Zou, and Rui Feng

Beyond MobileNet: An Improved MobileNet for Retinal Diseases 56
    Wenhui Zhu, Peijie Qiu, Xiwen Chen, Huayu Li, Hao Wang,
    Natasha Lepore, Oana M. Dumitrascu, and Yalin Wang

Prediction of Spherical Equivalent with Vanilla ResNet 66
    Huayu Li, Wenhui Zhu, Xiwen Chen, and Yalin Wang

Semi-supervised Learning for Myopic Maculopathy Analysis 75
    Jónathan Heras

A Clinically Guided Approach for Training Deep Neural Networks
for Myopic Maculopathy Classification 83
    Fabian Yii

Classification of Myopic Maculopathy Images with Self-supervised
Driven Multiple Instance Learning Network 95
    Jiawen Li, Jaehyeon Soon, Qilai Zhang, Qifan Zhang, and Yonghong He

Self-supervised Learning and Data Diversity Based Prediction of Spherical
Equivalent 106
   Di Liu, Li Wei, and Bo Yang

Myopic Maculopathy Analysis Using Multi-task Learning and Pseudo
Labeling 113
   Hyeonmin Kim and Hyeonseob Nam

Author Index 121

Automated Detection of Myopic Maculopathy in MMAC 2023: Achievements in Classification, Segmentation, and Spherical Equivalent Prediction

Yihao Li[1,2], Philippe Zhang[1,2,3], Yubo Tan[4], Jing Zhang[1,2], Zhihan Wang[1,2], Weili Jiang[5], Pierre-Henri Conze[1,6], Mathieu Lamard[1,2], Gwenolé Quellec[1], and Mostafa El Habib Daho[1,2(✉)]

[1] LaTIM UMR 1101, Inserm, Brest, France
mostafa.elhabibdaho@univ-brest.fr
[2] Univ Bretagne Occidentale, Brest, France
[3] Evolucare Technologies, Villers-Bretonneux, France
[4] University of Electronic Science and Technology of China, Chengdu, China
[5] College of Computer Science, Sichuan University, Chengdu, China
[6] IMT Atlantique, Brest, France

Abstract. Myopic macular degeneration is the most common complication of myopia and the primary cause of vision loss in individuals with pathological myopia. Early detection and prompt treatment are crucial in preventing vision impairment due to myopic maculopathy. This was the focus of the Myopic Maculopathy Analysis Challenge (MMAC), in which we participated. In task 1, classification of myopic maculopathy, we employed the contrastive learning framework, specifically SimCLR, to enhance classification accuracy by effectively capturing enriched features from unlabeled data. This approach not only improved the intrinsic understanding of the data but also elevated the performance of our classification model. For Task 2 (segmentation of myopic maculopathy plus lesions), we have developed independent segmentation models tailored for different lesion segmentation tasks and implemented a test-time augmentation strategy to further enhance the model's performance. As for Task 3 (prediction of spherical equivalent), we have designed a deep regression model based on the data distribution of the dataset and employed an integration strategy to enhance the model's prediction accuracy. The results we obtained are promising and have allowed us to position ourselves in the Top 6 of the classification task, the Top 2 of the segmentation task, and the Top 1 of the prediction task. The code is available at https://github.com/liyihao76/MMAC_LaTIM_Solution.

Keywords: Contrast Loss · Test-time Augmentation · Data Distribution · Ensemble Learning

B. Sheng et al. (Eds.): MICCAI 2023, LNCS 14563, pp. 1–17, 2024.
https://doi.org/10.1007/978-3-031-54857-4_1

1   Introduction

Myopia is a common eye disorder that affects millions of people worldwide [11]. It can develop into high myopia, leading to visual impairment, including blindness, due to the development of different types of myopic maculopathy [13,26]. Myopic maculopathy is especially prevalent in countries such as Japan, China, Denmark, and the United States [23,30]. The severity of myopic maculopathy can be classified into five categories [23]: no macular lesions, tessellated fundus, diffuse chorioretinal atrophy, patchy chorioretinal atrophy, and macular atrophy. Three additional "Plus" lesions are also defined and added to these categories: Lacquer Cracks (LC), Choroidal Neovascularization (CNV), and Fuchs Spot (FS). Early detection and treatment are essential for preventing vision loss in people with myopic maculopathy. However, the diagnosis of myopic maculopathy is limited by the time-consuming and labor-intensive process of manually inspecting images individually. Therefore, developing an effective computer-aided system for diagnosing myopic maculopathy is a promising area of research.

Deep learning (DL) methods have emerged as powerful tools in tackling challenges related to classification, segmentation, and prediction, demonstrating particular efficacy in medical imaging [17,20,21]. In ophthalmology, DL has catalyzed advancements in diagnosing eye diseases, including Diabetic Retinopathy (DR) [4,6,8] and myopia [19,31]. These recent studies have highlighted improvements in both the precision and efficiency of these diagnoses, underscoring the potential of DL in clinical applications.

Moreover, the field has seen innovative uses of abundant unlabeled data. Recognizing the cost and effort required for data labeling, researchers have pivoted towards self-supervised learning (SSL) approaches. These methods exploit unlabeled data for model pretraining in pretext tasks, subsequently applying them to target downstream tasks. This approach has proven effective in enhancing model performance and adaptability in various contexts [32,33].

Building upon these advancements in deep learning and the growing need for efficient, automated solutions in ophthalmology, the field has seen the inception of targeted initiatives like the Myopic Maculopathy Analysis Challenge (MMAC). The MMAC was organized to galvanize researchers worldwide to apply these innovative techniques in a focused setting. This challenge comprises three distinct tasks: (1) classification of myopic maculopathy, (2) segmentation of myopic maculopathy plus lesions, and (3) prediction of spherical equivalent, all utilizing a specially curated dataset of fundus images tailored to these tasks.

In alignment with these emerging trends and leveraging our expertise in deep learning, our team enthusiastically participated in all the tasks of this challenge. Our contributions were marked by notable achievements in each category:

- In the classification task (**6th place**), we employed SimCLR, a contrastive learning method, that allowed the model to learn richer representations from the data. The integration of ensemble strategies, particularly when paired with SimCLR, further enhanced the model's robustness.

– In the segmentation task (**2nd place**), we designed and tested independent models for different lesion segmentation tasks. In addition, the Test Time Augmentation strategy we used boosted the performance of the models.
– In regression task (**1st place**), we focused on the analysis of the distribution characteristics of the dataset and designed the experimental protocol according to the distribution law of the dataset so that the deep regression model can learn and reason in a targeted manner. Furthermore, incorporating the model ensemble strategy increases the accuracy of the prediction.

2   Materials and Methods

2.1   Datasets

The MMAC dataset is an extensive collection of color fundus images dedicated to research on myopic maculopathy. The dataset comprises fundus images gathered from various patients diagnosed with and without myopic maculopathy.

The sizes of each split of each task are summarized in Table 1. To maintain the challenge's integrity and fairness, both the validation and test datasets are securely held and not released to participants. The validation and testing phases are executed on the organizer's side to ensure unbiased evaluation.

The first Task (Classification of Myopic Maculopathy) is focused on a five-category image classification. The categories are as follows:

– Category 0: No macular lesions
– Category 1: Tessellated fundus
– Category 2: Diffuse chorioretinal atrophy
– Category 3: Patchy chorioretinal atrophy
– Category 4: Macular atrophy

The annotations were meticulously generated and reviewed manually by professional ophthalmologists. Two ophthalmologists annotated each image independently. In cases of discrepancies in labeling, a third senior ophthalmologist provided the final label. This rigorous process ensures the high quality and reliability of the dataset annotations.

The second Task (Segmentation of Myopic Maculopathy Plus Lesions) aims to segment three types of lesions:

– Lacquer Cracks (LC)
– Choroidal Neovascularization (CNV)
– Fuchs Spot (FS)

An ophthalmologist first performed the lesion annotations. A second ophthalmologist refined these annotations in consultation with the first. Both these ophthalmologists have over five years of experience. A senior ophthalmologist with a decade of experience in ophthalmology reviewed and finalized the annotations.

For the third Task (Prediction of Spherical Equivalent), the true value of the spherical equivalent (SE) was ascertained using the corneal curvature computer refractometer TOPCON KR-8900. The SE was computed as:

$$SE = S + \frac{1}{2}C \tag{1}$$

where S and C are the spherical and cylinder diopter, respectively; these values were acquired through the computer refractometer.

Table 1. Distribution of color fundus images for different tasks.

Task	Training Set	Validation Set	Test Set
Task1- Classification of myopic maculopathy	1143	248	915
Task2- Segmentation of myopic maculopathy plus lesions (Lacquer Cracks)	63	12	46
Task2- Segmentation of myopic maculopathy plus lesions (Choroidal Neovascularization)	32	7	22
Task2- Segmentation of myopic maculopathy plus lesions (Fuchs Spot)	54	13	45
Task3- Prediction of spherical equivalent	992	205	806

2.2 Task 1: Classification of Myopic Maculopathy

Several models were trialed for the classification task. These models included Resnet (18 and 50) [9], ViT [5], and Swin [22], among others. However, optimal results were achieved using a pipeline based on contrastive learning. This approach has recently gained traction for its ability to learn expressive representations from unlabeled data [33] [32]. Our implementation can be detailed as follows:

Pretext Task: Contrastive Learning Framework (SimCLR). As depicted in Fig. 1, our contrastive learning framework is rooted in the SimCLR architecture [3]. The essence of SimCLR is to maximize the agreement between various augmented views of the same data instance through a contrastive loss in the latent space. A detailed breakdown of the utilized augmentations is provided in Table 2. The architecture was supplemented with ResNet50 [9] as its backbone, known for its depth and performance prowess in image-related tasks.

Dataset Utilization: To make the most of the available data for the pretext unsupervised task, we amalgamated datasets from both Task 1 and Task 3. This approach not only broadened our data pool but also enabled the SimCLR model to capture a diverse range of features and representations.

Training Parameters: For training the SimCLR model, we standardized the image size to 256 × 256 pixels and utilized a batch size of 256. The temperature parameter was set at 0.07. Optimization was achieved using the AdamW

Table 2. Data augmentations for Task 1 and Task 3.

Operator	Parameters	Probability
Flip	horizontal, vertical	0.5
ShiftScaleRotate	shift_limit=0.2, scale_limit=0.1, rotate_limit=45	0.5
RandomBrightnessContrast	brightness_limit=0.2, contrast_limit=0.2	1.0
RandomGamma	gamma_limit=(80, 120)	1.0
CoarseDropout	max_height=5, min_height=1, max_width=512, min_width=51, max_holes=5	0.2
Sharpen	alpha=(0.2, 0.5), lightness=(0.5, 1.0)	1.0
Blur	blur_limit=3	1.0
Downscale	scale_min=0.7, scale_max=0.9	1.0

optimizer coupled with the OneCycleLR scheduler. The learning rate was maintained at 0.001, and weight decay was set at 2.3e–05. The training persisted for a total of 2,000 epochs, ensuring ample time for convergence and representation learning.

Downstream Task: Fine-Tuning. After the pretext task, we leveraged the learned representations for our primary objective, the classification of myopic maculopathy. For this supervised task, we fine-tuned the ResNet50 backbone extracted from the SimCLR architecture, excluding the projection head of SimCLR, which was discarded during this phase. The Task 1 dataset, accompanied by the provided labels, was employed for fine-tuning.

Checkpoint Strategy: To optimize our model's generalization, we employed a strategic checkpoint-saving approach. Checkpoints were saved based on various performance metrics, including Quadratic Weighted Kappa, Macro F1, and Macro Specificity. Additionally, a checkpoint capturing the average performance across these metrics was preserved. This strategy facilitated the eventual ensemble method, allowing for a harmonized prediction rooted in diverse evaluation criteria.

Test Stage: During the testing phase, we leaned into Test Time Augmentation (TTA) to enhance the robustness of our predictions. TTA has been shown to improve the generalization of models on unseen data. In conjunction with TTA, we employed an ensemble method drawing predictions from all saved checkpoints. This approach not only diversified our prediction source but also increased the reliability and accuracy of the final results.

2.3 Task 2: Segmentation of Myopic Maculopathy Plus Lesions

Segmentation of myopic maculopathy plus lesions in MMAC2023 is intended to detect pixel-level lesions, including LC, CNV, and FS. Table 1 illustrates that

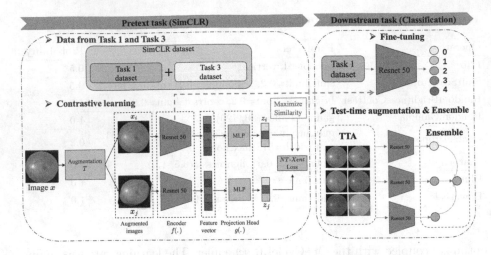

Fig. 1. Proposed pipeline for Task 1.

the datasets required for different lesion segmentation tasks are different. As a result, it is difficult to obtain a unified segmentation model through multi-task learning in order to segment different lesions. Three independent segmentation models were used for this purpose. For the purpose of achieving optimal lesion segmentation, a data augmentation strategy has been proposed for the training of models on small datasets while backbone selection is performed. The TTA strategy was also incorporated to enhance the model's robustness.

Data Split and Augmentation. As with the Diabetic Retinopathy Analysis Challenge (DRAC) [24], the segmentation tasks focus on the segmentation of lesions at the pixel level of 2D images, and there are a limited number of patients in the dataset. Following the best segmentation implementation [16] in the DRAC challenge, we used all of the training data from the challenge to train our model. The data augmentation strategy outlined in Table 3 was employed to avoid overfitting problems. The model will not encounter any original training samples due to the use of geometric transforms and pixel-wise transformations, which generate diverse input representations [16].

Backbone Selection. During the validation phase of the challenge, we extensively tested different segmentation backbones in order to determine the optimal one. Testing was conducted using Unet++ [35], MAnet [7], Linknet [1], FPN [15], PSPNet [34], DeepLabV3+ [2] and U^2-Net [25] with the encoder of ResNet [10] or EfficientNet [28] architectures.

Table 3. Data augmentations for Task 2.

Operator	Parameters	Probability
Flip	horizontal, vertical	0.5
ShiftScaleRotate	shift_limit=0.2, scale_limit=0.1, rotate_limit=90	0.5
RandomBrightnessContrast	brightness_limit=0.2, contrast_limit=0.2	1.0
RandomGamma	gamma_limit=(80, 120)	1.0
Sharpen	alpha=(0.2, 0.5), lightness=(0.5, 1.0)	1.0
Blur	blur_limit=3	1.0
Downscale	scale_min=0.7, scale_max=0.9	1.0
GridDistortion	num steps=5, distort limit=0.3	0.2
CoarseDropout	max_height=128, min_height=32, max_width=128, min_width=32, max_holes=3	0.2

TTA. The robustness of the model was improved by using TTA during inference. Each color fundus image was rotated by 90°, 180°, and 270° and then used in conjunction with the original image as input to the model. The final inference image was obtained by averaging the four different inference results after their restoration.

2.4   Task 3: Prediction of Spherical Equivalent

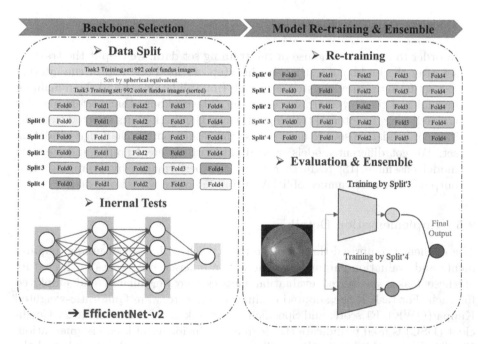

Fig. 2. Proposed workflow for Task 3. Gray folds represent the training set (internal), the validation set (internal) by green folds, and the test set (internal) by yellow folds. (Color figure online)

The prediction of spherical equivalent can assist in diagnosing the risk of myopic maculopathy associated with increased degrees of myopia [30]. Considering that there is a limited number of images in the training set and a limited number of submissions in the validation phase, we proposed the workflow shown in Fig. 2. The following steps were tested for the prediction of spherical equivalent:

(1) Backbone Selection

To determine which backbone is most effective for the prediction task, we used five-fold cross-validation on the training set to assess various backbones' overall performance. In order to ensure a balanced data distribution, we sorted the data according to spherical equivalent values from smallest to largest. The training set of the challenge was split into three sets using five-fold cross-validation: an internal training set (3 folds), an internal validation set (1 fold), and an internal test set (1 fold).
Testing was performed on VGG [27], ResNet [10], DenseNet [12], EfficientNet [28], and EfficientNetV2 [29] architectures. The internal training set was used for training the model, the checkpoint was selected based on the R-Square value of the internal validation set, and the mean of the R-Square on the internal test of Split(0–4) was calculated to represent its overall performance. The list of data augmentation strategies is described in Table 2.

(2) Model Re-training & Ensemble

In order to maximize the use of the training set data, we resplit the training set after the backbone testing. In this step, we used one fold of the internal test set from the previous step as the internal validation set and the remaining four folds as the new internal training set. The backbone that performs well is trained using the internal training set, while the checkpoints selected from the internal validation set are used to test the results on the challenge validation set. We got different models by training with different splits, and we used model ensemble [18] to further boost the performance by averaging their outputs. The performance of TTA during inference was also tested.

2.5   Implementation Details

The challenge comprised three diverse tasks, each with a set of unique requirements and evaluation parameters. Due to the inherent differences in the nature of these tasks, specialized evaluation metrics were formulated and employed for each. For task 1, the adopted evaluation indicators are Quadratic-weighted Kappa (QWK), F1 score, and Specificity. For task 2, the Dice Similarity Coefficient (DSC) is used to indicate the degree of coincidence of lesion segmentation. Finally, for the third task, the coefficient of determination R-squared, and the Mean Absolute Error (MAE) are employed to evaluate label regression's degree of correlation and distance.

Table 4. Implementation details used in experiments.

Implementation	Task1	Task2	Task3
Preprocessing	None	Normalize(mean=(0,0,0), std=(1,1,1))	
Input size	512×512 pixels	800×800 pixels	
Backbone	ResNet50	MAnet (Encoder: ResNet34)	EfficientNet-v2 (tf_EfficientNetv2_l)
Library	timm	SMP	timm
Pretrained weights	Pretext Task	Imagenet	Imagenet
Loss	CrossEntropyLoss	DiceLoss+CrossEntropyLoss	SmoothL1Loss
Optimizer	AdamW		
Learning rate	1e−3 (OneCycleLR scheduler)	1e−4 (w/o scheduler)	2e-w/o scheduler)
Weight decay	2.3e−05	1e−2	1e−2
Augmentation	see Table 2	see Table 3	see Table 2
Batch size	8	5	6
Epochs	200	1000	800
Train/Val split	0.8:0.2	1:0	0.8:0.2
Metric	QWK, Macro F1, Macro Specificity	Dice	R-squared

In terms of computational infrastructure, the models and algorithms were implemented on a high-performance machine boasting 196 GB of RAM. The Nvidia GPU Tesla V100s with 32 GB memory and NVIDIA A6000 with 48 GB memory were employed to facilitate the intense calculations demanded by deep learning tasks. The software ecosystem was primarily built around PyTorch, a leading deep learning framework. Additional libraries like Timm (known for its efficient training routines and pre-trained models), Segmentation Models PyTorch (SMP) for the segmentation task, and Lightly for contrastive learning were incorporated to provide a robust and efficient system for the challenge's requirements.

Table 4 provides a brief description of our operators and detailed parameters for training. Unless otherwise specified, all experiments are conducted using reported configurations and parameters.

3 Results

3.1 Task 1: Classification of Myopic Maculopathy

Among the backbones we tested for classifying myopic maculopathy, ResNet50 delivered the most promising results, as presented in Table 6. This superior performance prompted us to delve deeper into optimizing ResNet50 further. During this optimization, we integrated SimCLR as a Pretext task. The added value of SimCLR to our pipeline was evident, as demonstrated by the improved results compared to Resnet50 without a pretext task. This suggests that SimCLR effectively captures enhanced representations from unlabeled data, thus enriching our model's features and subsequently elevating its performance. Following this, the model was fine-tuned on the Task 1 dataset.

Further extending the model's capabilities, we experimented with several ensemble strategies:

- Mean: The strategy involved selecting the classifier that showcased the best mean performance across the three metrics based on the validation set during training.
- All: This method calculated the mean of the logits outputs of each model before the Argmax operation, capturing a holistic insight from all models.
- Majority: A majority voting approach, this strategy collated predictions based on the predominant class predicted by all classifiers.

Upon integrating ensemble strategies with ResNet50 optimized using SimCLR, we observed significant improvements in performance. The 'Majority' ensemble strategy combined with SimCLR achieved the highest Macro_F1 score of 0.8176 and an overall score of 0.8881. Interestingly, the 'All' strategy demonstrated the peak QWK (0.9080) and Specificity (0.9427), emphasizing its capacity to capture comprehensive insights from the models. The ensemble method 'Mean' also displayed commendable results, with an overall score reaching 0.8781 when combined with SimCLR. It's evident from the data that the addition of ensemble strategies, particularly in tandem with SimCLR, significantly boosts the model's performance across various metrics (Table 5).

Table 5. Task 1 validation results using different strategies

Backbone	Ensemble	TTA	Pretext	QWK	Macro_F1	Specificity	score
Rexnet200	✕	✕	✕	0.7524	0.5873	0.9126	0.7508
Swin	✕	✕	✕	0.8159	0.6449	0.9155	0.7921
Resnet18	✕	✕	✕	0.8721	0.6857	0.9236	0.8271
Resnet50	✕	✕	✕	0.8845	0.7491	0.9315	0.8550
Resnet50	Mean	✕	SimCLR	0.9030	0.7926	0.9388	0.8781
Resnet50	Majority	✕	SimCLR	0.9067	**0.8176**	0.9400	**0.8881**
Resnet50	All	✕	SimCLR	**0.9080**	0.7954	**0.9427**	0.8821
Resnet50	Majority	✓	SimCLR	0.9028	0.8049	0.9385	0.8821

As requested by the organizers, we submitted our four best-performing versions of our solutions for the final test, with these models being evaluated on a new, unseen dataset. Referring to Table 6, we notice a slight decline in scores from validation to test phases, a common phenomenon due to the nuances of real-world data that may not be entirely captured in the validation set. The highest test scores were achieved using ResNet50 with the Majority ensemble method and TTA. This consistency from validation to test suggests that our methods are robust and not merely overfitting to the validation set.

Table 6. The performance of the different solution versions in Task 1 during the validation and testing phases

Phase	Ver.	Backbone	Ensemble	TTA	Pretext	QWK	Macro_F1	Specificity	score
Validation	(1)	Resnet50	Majority	✗	SimCLR	0.9067	**0.8176**	0.9400	**0.8881**
	(2)	Resnet50	Majority	✓	SimCLR	0.9028	0.8049	0.9385	0.8821
	(3)	Resnet50	All	✗	SimCLR	**0.9080**	0.7954	**0.9427**	0.8821
	(4)	Resnet50	Mean	✗	SimCLR	0.9030	0.7926	0.9388	0.8781
Test	(1)	Resnet50	Majority	✗	SimCLR	0.8811	0.7071	0.9373	0.8419
	(2)	Resnet50	Majority	✓	SimCLR	**0.8858**	**0.7081**	0.9396	**0.8445**
	(3)	Resnet50	All	✗	SimCLR	0.8856	0.7044	**0.9409**	0.8437
	(4)	Resnet50	Mean	✗	SimCLR	0.8677	0.6942	0.9370	0.8330

Table 7. Results of Task 2 backbone selection on the validation set.

Backbone	Encoder	LC DSC	CNV DSC	FS DSC	Avg DSC
UNet++	EfficientNet-b0	0.7030	0.5458	0.7741	0.6743
UNet++	EfficientNet-b1	0.6748	0.5913	0.7866	0.6842
UNet++	EfficientNet-b2	0.7081	0.5990	0.7881	0.6984
UNet++	EfficientNet-b3	0.7158	0.5516	0.7393	0.6689
UNet++	EfficientNet-b4	0.7087	0.6257	0.7123	0.6823
UNet++	EfficientNet-b5	0.7051	0.5890	0.7956	0.6966
UNet++	EfficientNet-b6	0.7203	0.5148	0.7940	0.6764
UNet++	EfficientNet-b7	0.6829	0.5895	0.8068	0.6931
UNet++	ResNet34	0.7303	0.6339	0.8167	0.7270
UNet++	ResNet50	0.7216	0.4165	0.8068	0.6483
UNet++	ResNet101	0.7046	0.6064	0.7685	0.6932
UNet++	ResNet152	0.7055	0.5331	0.8306	0.6897
DeepLabV3+	ResNet34	0.6986	0.6351	0.8347	0.7228
FPN	ResNet34	0.6969	0.5891	0.7769	0.6877
Linknet	ResNet34	0.7304	0.5385	0.7974	0.6888
PSPNet	ResNet34	0.7065	0.3974	0.7908	0.6316
MAnet	ResNet34	0.7573	**0.6885**	**0.8498**	**0.7652**
U^2-Net	-	**0.7651**	0.3877	0.7717	0.6415

3.2 Task 2: Segmentation of Myopic Maculopathy Plus Lesions

During the validation phase of the MMAC Challenge, we tested the performance of different backbones and encoders on the validation set, as shown in Table 7. Based on the UNet++ structure, we compared the performance of ResNet and EfficientNet encoders. The ResNet34 encoder performed the best among them, and we used it to test the performance of other architectures. The segmentation of LC lesions using U^2-Net was found to be the most accurate, followed by segmentation using MAnet. MAnet demonstrated the best performance for segmenting both CNV lesions and FS lesions.

Table 8. The performance of the different solution versions in Task 2 during the validation and testing phases.

Phase	Ver.	Model LC	Model CNV	Model FS	TTA	LC DSC	CNV DSC	FS DSC	Avg DSC
Validation	(1)	U^2-Net	MAnet	MAnet	✗	**0.7651**	**0.6885**	**0.8498**	**0.7678**
	(2)	U^2-Net	MAnet	MAnet	✓	0.7367	0.6563	0.8024	0.7318
	(3)	MAnet	MAnet	MAnet	✗	0.7573	0.6885	0.8498	0.7652
	(4)	MAnet	MAnet	MAnet	✓	0.7563	0.6563	0.8024	0.7383
Test	(1)	U^2-Net	MAnet	MAnet	✗	0.6403	0.6250	0.8215	0.6956
	(2)	U^2-Net	MAnet	MAnet	✓	0.6682	0.6557	0.8348	0.7196
	(3)	MAnet	MAnet	MAnet	✗	0.6658	0.6250	0.8215	0.7041
	(4)	MAnet	MAnet	MAnet	✓	**0.6838**	**0.6557**	**0.8348**	**0.7248**

Based on the results of the backbone tests, we selected the four best-performing versions as the solutions submitted in the testing phase of the challenge, as shown in Table 8. The Ver. (1) combines the excellent performance of U^2-Net and MAnet on different segmentation tasks, thus performing well during the validation phase. Unfortunately, U^2-Net suffers from the overfitting problem due to the limited number of patients in datasets and therefore, performs poorly in the testing phase. Additionally, the tests indicate that the TTA approach significantly improves the robustness of the model and boosts the segmentation performance of the different submission versions in the testing phase. As a result, we found that the MAnet-based model with TTA strategy submission (Ver. (4)) performed optimally, with dice of 0.6838 for LC lesions segmentation, 0.6557 for CNV lesions segmentation, and 0.8348 for FS lesions segmentation on the test set. Figure 3 illustrates the performance of our MAnet-based model on different lesion segmentation tasks. Our model demonstrates proficiency in segmenting smaller lesions, as depicted in Fig. 3(a), but it shows limitations in accurately segmenting larger or more complex lesions, as observed in Fig. 3(b).

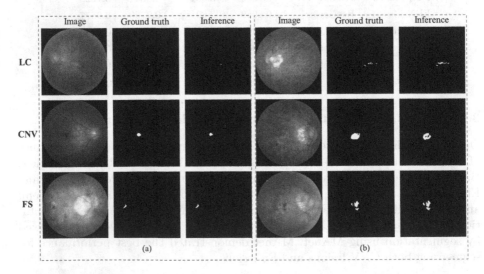

Fig. 3. Segmentation performance of MAnet on the validation set of Task 2.

3.3   Task 3: Prediction of Spherical Equivalent

Table 9. R-Squared results of Task 3 with backbone selection on the internal test set.

Backbone(Timm)	Split0	Split1	Split2	Split3	Split4	Avg.
vgg11	0.6773	0.7179	0.6808	0.6663	0.6241	0.6733
vgg16	0.5915	0.6507	0.6821	0.7699	0.6753	0.6739
resnet50	0.7061	0.7469	0.7328	0.6976	0.6843	0.7135
resnet152	0.7079	0.6972	0.6768	0.7112	0.7048	0.6996
resnet200d	0.7761	0.7675	0.7300	0.7494	0.7274	0.7501
densenet121	0.7077	0.7289	0.6821	0.7303	0.7057	0.7109
densenet161	0.7543	0.6865	0.7094	0.7449	0.7337	0.7258
densenet169	0.7416	0.7367	0.7166	0.7285	0.7410	0.7329
densenet201	0.7405	0.7347	0.7094	0.7172	0.762	0.7328
efficientnet_b0	0.7318	0.7446	0.7129	0.7384	0.7472	0.7350
efficientnet_b1	0.7108	0.7136	0.7084	0.7098	0.7535	0.7192
efficientnet_b2	0.7282	0.6952	0.7027	0.7554	0.7486	0.7260
tf_efficientnet_b6	0.7443	0.7918	0.7098	0.8264	0.7272	0.7599
tf_efficientnet_b7	0.7728	0.7954	0.7453	0.7868	0.7787	0.7758
tf_efficientnet_b8	0.7980	0.8043	0.8170	0.8581	0.7686	0.8092
tf_efficientnetv2_s	0.7765	0.7746	0.7206	0.8069	0.7520	0.7661
tf_efficientnetv2_l	0.8147	0.8374	0.7801	0.8226	0.8336	**0.8177**
tf_efficientnetv2_xl	0.8115	0.8354	0.8005	0.8006	0.8166	0.8129

In order to evaluate the overall performance of different backbones on the internal test set, we first tested our proposed five-fold cross-validation method as shown in Table 9. In light of the mean values of R-Squared across different Split internal test sets, we selected three backbones that provided a better performance: tf_efficientnetv2_l, tf_efficientnetv2_xl, and tf_efficientnet_b8. As the organizer's Python Packages currently do not support the current implementation of tf_efficientnetv2_xl, we chose to use tf_efficientnetv2_l and tf_efficientnet_b8 as backbones.

The dataset was resplit and then tf_efficientnetv2_l and tf_efficientnet_b8 were trained. As shown in Table 10, some models that performed well on the new internal validation set were evaluated on the validation set of the competition. Based on the results, it can be seen that the tf_efficientnet_b8 model obtained by Split'1 training and the tf_efficientnetv2_l model obtained by Split'2/Split'3/Split'4 perform well on the validation set. These models are then ensembled. Our model ensemble methods performed well in both the validation and testing phases, improving prediction accuracy without overfitting. As a result of ensemble tf_efficientnetv2_l (Split' 3) and tf_efficientnetv2_l (Split' 4), the solution Ver. (3) obtained an R2 value of 0.8735 and an MAE value of 0.7080 on the test set.

Table 10. The performance of the different solution versions in Task 3 during the validation and testing phases.

Phase	Ver.	Ensemble	Model(Split)	TTA	R-Squared	MAE
Validation	–	✗	tf_efficientnet_b8(Split' 1)	✗	0.8230	0.6818
	–	✗	tf_efficientnetv2_l(Split' 2)	✗	0.8526	0.6723
	(1)	✗	tf_efficientnetv2_l(Split' 3)	✗	0.8622	0.6299
	–	✗	tf_efficientnetv2_l(Split' 3)	✓	0.8617	0.6307
	–	✗	tf_efficientnetv2_l(Split' 4)	✗	0.8539	0.6570
	(2)	✓	tf_efficientnet_b8(Split' 1)+ tf_efficientnetv2_l(Split' 3)	✓	0.8669	0.6254
	(3)	✓	tf_efficientnetv2_l(Split' 3)+ tf_efficientnetv2_l(Split' 4)	✗	0.8734	**0.6073**
	–	✓	tf_efficientnetv2_l(Split' 3)+ tf_efficientnetv2_l(Split' 4)	✓	0.8705	0.6109
	(4)	✓	tf_efficientnetv2_l(Split' 2)+ tf_efficientnetv2_l(Split' 3)+ tf_efficientnetv2_l(Split' 4)	✗	**0.8745**	0.6075
Test	(1)	✗	tf_efficientnetv2_l(Split' 3)	✗	0.8507	0.7627
	(2)	✓	tf_efficientnet_b8(Split' 1)+ tf_efficientnetv2_l(Split' 3)	✓	0.8714	0.7258
	(3)	✓	tf_efficientnetv2_l(Split' 3)+ tf_efficientnetv2_l(Split' 4)	✗	**0.8735**	0.7080
	(4)	✓	tf_efficientnetv2_l(Split' 2)+ tf_efficientnetv2_l(Split' 3)+ tf_efficientnetv2_l(Split' 4)	✗	0.8732	**0.7041**

4   Discussion and Conclusions

In this work, we presented our solutions for three tasks in the MMAC Challenge. For Task 1, ResNet50 emerged as the backbone of choice for classification. Its performance was substantially amplified upon incorporating SimCLR, a pretext task that effectively harnessed unlabeled data to enrich model representations. A deeper exploration of ensemble strategies, particularly the 'Majority' and 'All' methods, revealed significant performance boosts. These findings were validated on an unseen dataset, where our models demonstrated robustness, with the ResNet50 combined with the Majority ensemble method and TTA showcasing impressive consistency. For the final test rank in this task, our model secured the 8th position.

Segmentation of myopic maculopathy plus lesions (Task 2) provided its own set of challenges. The UNet++ structure fortified with ResNet34 encoder showcased promising results. However, a key revelation was the susceptibility of the U^2-Net model to overfitting, especially with limited datasets. Despite this setback, the MAnet-based model, augmented with the TTA strategy, emerged triumphant, achieving stellar dice scores for various lesion segmentations. This excellence in segmentation led our model to be ranked 2nd in the challenge.

The prediction of the spherical equivalent (Task 3) pivoted on our utilization of the tf_efficientnetv2_l and tf_efficientnet_b8 backbones, with the latter especially excelling in the validation phase. Embracing model ensembling further elevated our performance metrics. Notably, the ensemble of tf_efficientnetv2_l models derived from specific data splits yielded exceptional results on the test dataset, catapulting us to the top position for this task.

It should be noted that more models deserve further testing. As part of Task 3, we identified some backbone network architectures that performed well. However, we were unable to complete the tests due to limitations in the Python Packages provided by the organizer. Furthermore, nnUNet [14] is a common segmentation solution used in medical competitions. In light of the positive results achieved by nnUNet in the DRAC Challenge [20], it raises the possibility that nnUNet can also perform well in the MMAC Challenge.

Acknowledgements. The work was conducted in the framework of the ANR RHU project Evired. This work benefited from state aid managed by the French National Research Agency under the "Investissement d'Avenir" program, reference ANR-18-RHUS-0008.

References

1. Chaurasia, A., Culurciello, E.: Linknet: Exploiting encoder representations for efficient semantic segmentation. In: 2017 IEEE Visual Communications and Image Processing (VCIP), pp. 1–4. IEEE (2017)
2. Chen, L.C., Zhu, Y., Papandreou, G., Schroff, F., Adam, H.: Encoder-decoder with atrous separable convolution for semantic image segmentation. In: Proceedings of the European Conference on Computer Vision (ECCV), pp. 801–818 (2018)
3. Chen, T., Kornblith, S., Norouzi, M., Hinton, G.: A simple framework for contrastive learning of visual representations. In: Proceedings of the 37th International Conference on Machine Learning, ICML'20, JMLR.org (2020)
4. Dai, L., et al.: A deep learning system for detecting diabetic retinopathy across the disease spectrum. Nat. Commun. **12**(1), 3242 (2021)
5. Dosovitskiy, A., et al.: An image is worth 16x16 words: transformers for image recognition at scale. CoRR abs/2010.11929 (2020). https://arxiv.org/abs/2010.11929
6. El Habib Daho, M., et al.: Improved automatic diabetic retinopathy severity classification using deep multimodal fusion of UWF-CFP and OCTA images. In: Antony, B., Chen, H., Fang, H., Fu, H., Lee, C.S., Zheng, Y. (eds.) Ophthalmic Medical Image Analysis. OMIA 2023. LNCS, vol. 14096, pp. 11–20. Springer, Cham (2023). https://doi.org/10.1007/978-3-031-44013-7_2
7. Fan, T., Wang, G., Li, Y., Wang, H.: Ma-net: A multi-scale attention network for liver and tumor segmentation. IEEE Access **8**, 179656–179665 (2020)
8. Gwenolé, Q., Hassan, A.H., Mathieu, L., Pierre-Henri, C., Pascale, M., Béatrice, C.: Explain: explanatory artificial intelligence for diabetic retinopathy diagnosis. Med. Image Anal. **72** (2021). https://doi.org/10.1016/j.media.2021.102118

9. He, K., Zhang, X., Ren, S., Sun, J.: Deep residual learning for image recognition. CoRR abs/1512.03385 (2015). https://arxiv.org/abs/1512.03385
10. He, K., Zhang, X., Ren, S., Sun, J.: Deep residual learning for image recognition. In: Proceedings of the IEEE Conference on Computer Vision and Pattern Recognition, pp. 770–778 (2016)
11. Holden, B.A., et al.: Global prevalence of myopia and high myopia and temporal trends from 2000 through 2050. Ophthalmology **123**(5), 1036–1042 (2016)
12. Huang, G., Liu, Z., Van Der Maaten, L., Weinberger, K.Q.: Densely connected convolutional networks. In: Proceedings of the IEEE Conference on Computer Vision and Pattern Recognition, pp. 4700–4708 (2017)
13. Ikuno, Y.: Overview of the complications of high myopia. Retina **37**(12), 2347–2351 (2017)
14. Isensee, F., Jaeger, P.F., Kohl, S.A., Petersen, J., Maier-Hein, K.H.: nnU-net: a self-configuring method for deep learning-based biomedical image segmentation. Nat. Methods **18**(2), 203–211 (2021)
15. Kirillov, A., He, K., Girshick, R., Dollár, P.: A unified architecture for instance and semantic segmentation. In: CVPR (2017)
16. Kwon, G., Kim, E., Kim, S., Bak, S., Kim, M., Kim, J.: Bag of tricks for developing diabetic retinopathy analysis framework to overcome data scarcity. In: Sheng, B., Aubreville, M. (eds.) Mitosis Domain Generalization and Diabetic Retinopathy Analysis. MIDOG DRAC 2022 2022. LNCS, vol. 13597, pp. 59–73. Springer, Cham (2023). https://doi.org/10.1007/978-3-031-33658-4_7
17. Lahsaini, I., El Habib Daho, M., Chikh, M.A.: Deep transfer learning based classification model for covid-19 using chest CT-scans. Pattern Recogn. Lett. **152**, 122–128 (2023). https://doi.org/10.1016/j.patrec.2021.08.035
18. Lakshminarayanan, B., Pritzel, A., Blundell, C.: Simple and scalable predictive uncertainty estimation using deep ensembles. In: Advances in Neural Information Processing Systems, vol. 30 (2017)
19. Li, L.F., et al.: Deep learning system to predict the 5-year risk of high myopia using fundus imaging in children. NPJ Digit. Med. **6**(10) (2023). https://doi.org/10.1038/s41746-023-00752-8
20. Li, Y., et al.: Segmentation, classification, and quality assessment of UW-OCTA images for the diagnosis of diabetic retinopathy. In: Sheng, B., Aubreville, M. (eds.) Mitosis Domain Generalization and Diabetic Retinopathy Analysis. MIDOG DRAC 2022 2022. LNCS, vol. 13597, pp. 146–160. Springer, Cham (2023). https://doi.org/10.1007/978-3-031-33658-4_14
21. Liu, R., et al.: Deepdrid: diabetic retinopathy-grading and image quality estimation challenge. Patterns **3**(6), 100512 (2022)
22. Liu, Z., et al.: Swin transformer: Hierarchical vision transformer using shifted windows. CoRR abs/2103.14030 (2021). https://arxiv.org/abs/2103.14030
23. Ohno-Matsui, K., et al.: International photographic classification and grading system for myopic maculopathy. Am. J. Ophthalmol. **159**(5), 877–883 (2015)
24. Qian, B., et al.: Drac: diabetic retinopathy analysis challenge with ultra-wide optical coherence tomography angiography images. arXiv preprint arXiv:2304.02389 (2023)
25. Qin, X., Zhang, Z., Huang, C., Dehghan, M., Zaiane, O.R., Jagersand, M.: U2-net: Going deeper with nested u-structure for salient object detection. Pattern Recogn. **106**, 107404 (2020)
26. Silva, R.: Myopic maculopathy: a review. Ophthalmologica **228**(4), 197–213 (2012)
27. Simonyan, K., Zisserman, A.: Very deep convolutional networks for large-scale image recognition. arXiv preprint arXiv:1409.1556 (2014)

28. Tan, M., Le, Q.: Efficientnet: Rethinking model scaling for convolutional neural networks. In: International Conference on Machine Learning, pp. 6105–6114. PMLR (2019)
29. Tan, M., Le, Q.: Efficientnetv2: Smaller models and faster training. In: International Conference on Machine Learning, pp. 10096–10106. PMLR (2021)
30. Yokoi, T., Ohno-Matsui, K.: Diagnosis and treatment of myopic maculopathy. Asia-Pacific J. Ophthalmol. **7**(6), 415–421 (2018)
31. Yue, Z., et al.: Performances of artificial intelligence in detecting pathologic myopia: a systematic review and meta-analysis. Eye (2023). https://doi.org/10.1038/s41433-023-02551-7
32. Zeghlache, R., et al.: Longitudinal self-supervised learning using neural ordinary differential equation. In: Rekik, I., Adeli, E., Park, S.H., Cintas, C., Zamzmi, G. (eds.) Predictive Intelligence in Medicine. PRIME 2023. LNCS, vol. 14277, pp. 1–13. Springer, Cham (2023). https://doi.org/10.1007/978-3-031-46005-0_1
33. Zeghlache, R. et al.: Detection of Diabetic Retinopathy Using Longitudinal Self-supervised Learning. In: Antony, B., Fu, H., Lee, C.S., MacGillivray, T., Xu, Y., Zheng, Y. (eds.) Ophthalmic Medical Image Analysis. OMIA 2022. LNCS, vol. 13576, pp. 43–52. Springer, Cham (2022). https://doi.org/10.1007/978-3-031-16525-2_5
34. Zhao, H., Shi, J., Qi, X., Wang, X., Jia, J.: Pyramid scene parsing network. In: Proceedings of the IEEE Conference on Computer Vision and Pattern Recognition, pp. 2881–2890 (2017)
35. Zhou, Z., Rahman Siddiquee, M.M., Tajbakhsh, N., Liang, J.: UNet++: a nested u-net architecture for medical image segmentation. In: Stoyanov, D., et al. (eds.) DLMIA/ML-CDS -2018. LNCS, vol. 11045, pp. 3–11. Springer, Cham (2018). https://doi.org/10.1007/978-3-030-00889-5_1

Swin-MMC: Swin-Based Model for Myopic Maculopathy Classification in Fundus Images

Li Lu[1], Xuhao Pan[2], Panji Jin[1], and Ye Ding[1(✉)]

[1] School of Computer Science and Technology, Dongguan University of Technology, Dongguan 523808, China
{221115220,dingye}@dgut.edu.cn, 1340880735@qq.com
[2] School of Statistics and Information, Shanghai University of International Business and Economics, Shanghai 201620, China

Abstract. Myopic maculopathy is a highly myopic retinal disorder that often occurs in highly myopic patients, serving as a major cause of visual impairment and blindness in numerous countries. Currently, fundus images serve as a prevalent diagnostic tool for myopic maculopathy. However, its efficacy relies on the expertise of clinicians, making the process labor-intensive. Thus, we propose a model specifically designed for the image classification of myopic maculopathy, named Swin-MMC, based on the Swin Transformer model architecture, which achieves outstanding performance on the test dataset. To achieve a finer-grained classification of myopic maculopathy in fundus images, we have innovatively and for the first time proposed the use of enhanced ArcFace loss in medical image classification. Then, based on the Swin-MMC model, we introduce a weak label strategy that effectively mitigates overfitting. Our approach achieves significantly improved results on the test dataset and can be easily used for various datasets and classification tasks. We conduct a series of experiments in the MMAC2023 challenge. In the testing phase, our average performance metric reaches 86.60%. In the further testing phase, our model's performance improves to 88.23%, ultimately securing the championship in the MMAC2023 challenge. The codes allowing replication of this study have been made publicly available at https://github.com/LuliDreamAI/MICCAI_TASK1.

Keywords: Medical image classification · Myopic maculopathy · Fundus images

1 Introduction

Myopic maculopathy stands as one of the most severe threats to global visual health, also known as myopic maculopathy degeneration [9]. In numerous regions, myopic maculopathy degeneration serves as a prominent cause of visual impairment and blindness. Moreover, the application scope of fundus images is remarkably extensive, they not only assist in the treatment of age-related macular degeneration (AMD) [17] but also are employed in the detection and screening of glaucoma [23] while playing a crucial role in the identification and classification of diabetic retinopathy (DR) [2]. Medical practitioners diagnose the presence of myopic maculopathy through color fundus images or aim to prevent its further deterioration [16, 21]. In the field of medicine, determining whether an individual is afflicted with myopic maculopathy often requires specialized ophthalmologists to meticulously examine images. This process not only consumes a substantial amount of manpower and time but is also relatively slow. However, with the advancement of artificial intelligence (AI), deep learning plays a crucial role in automating clinical data processing, it is now possible to discern the presence of macular lesions in fundus images without the need for extensive human resources and time investment [14].

In the early stages, the detection of ocular diseases primarily relied on the binary classification of fundus images, which merely distinguished between abnormal and normal images. With the advancement of deep neural network technologies, Khan et al. [11] combined popular models ResNet50 and InceptionResNetV2 to create an ensemble model, achieving an accuracy of 86.08% in binary classification tasks. Chen et al. [3] enhanced accuracy to 90.56% in binary datasets by introducing hybrid units in the dense layer. However, due to the complexity of ocular structures, the classification of fundus images in recent years has moved beyond simply separating pathological from normal images. It now focuses more on finer and more precise categorizations of fundus pathologies and classifications of various types of ocular diseases. Liu et al. [8] focused their research on developing a model based on the Vision Transformer (ViT) [6], aimed at classifying a dataset containing a diverse range of abnormal images. These abnormalities may originate from any of six different ocular diseases, including age-related macular degeneration, diabetes, and glaucoma, among others. The study employed Vision Transformers of varying layer counts, with the objective of achieving accurate classification across seven distinct labels (healthy and six different diseases). Utilizing a 14-layer Vision Transformer model, the model demonstrated optimal performance, evidenced by an F1-score of 83.49%, sensitivity of 84.00%, precision of 83.00%, and a Kappa score of 0.802. However, it is noteworthy that the study did not venture into a more detailed subdivision within each disease category. Compared to professional ophthalmologists, AI models based on deep neural networks have shown exceptional efficiency and outstanding performance in large-scale medical analysis [7]. Therefore, exploring how to efficiently apply neural network models for more precise classification of ocular diseases represents a highly pertinent direction. Additionally, several deep learning algorithms have already been effectively utilized for screening and classification tasks related to diabetic retinopathy [4, 12, 18] and glaucoma [15, 20].

To address the classification of the myopic maculopathy problem, Sun et al. [19] proposed a feature fusion framework that comprises a prior knowledge extraction module and a feature fusion module, and the model achieves an AUC value of 0.998 on the test dataset. Wang et al. [21] developed a deep learning model for detection and classification and achieved high sensitivities, specificities,

and reliable Cohen's kappa. In recent years, with the popularity of Vision Transformer [6] and Swin Transformer [13], many researchers and scholars began to use
them widely. Hossain et al. [10] proposed the Swin-FSR model, which employs
the Swin Transformer with spatial and depth-wise attention mechanisms for
fundus image super-resolution. This ensures that important fine details are preserved during the compression and decompression processes of super-resolved
images. The ViT is commonly employed in medical image classification and segmentation. However, the performance of ViT significantly deteriorates when subjected to adversarial attacks. Almalik et al. [1] introduced a novel self-ensembling
approach to enhance the robustness of the ViT model against adversarial attacks.
The structure of Swin Transformer is shown in Fig. 1, where SwinTB represents
Swin Transformer blocks. Transformer-based models have surpassed traditional
Convolutional Neural Network (CNN) architectures in many image classification
tasks. Considering computational resources and inference speed, we choose the
Swin-base as our baseline model. Building on the Swin Transformer model, we
introduce a novel classification model named Swin-MMC to specifically address
myopic maculopathy classification. The performance details of Swin-MMC will
be discussed in the next section.

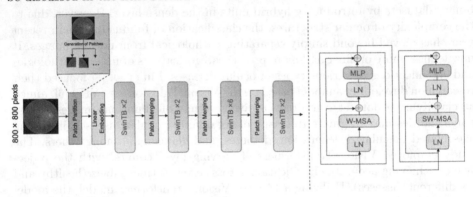

Fig. 1. The architecture of a Swin Transformer (Swin-base).

In this paper, our primary contributions are summarized as follows:

- We propose a Swin-based framework, named Swin-MMC, that is adaptive to
  medical image classification and demonstrates superior performance on the
  test dataset.
- We use the enhanced ArcFace loss with 3 sub-centers (En-ArcFace loss) as
  the model's loss function for the first time in classification tasks in the field
  of medical image processing.
- We design a weak label strategy based on our Swin-MMC model that can
  generate high-quality weak labels and make inferences efficiently simultaneously.

The rest of this paper is organized as follows. In Sect. 2, we will provide
a detailed introduction to our classification method. Next, in Sect. 3, we will
provide a detailed introduction to the dataset, as well as specific details about

the implementation of the experiments. Then, in Sect. 4, we will discuss the results and the ablation study, as well as our future work. Finally, in Sect. 5, we will conclude the paper.

2 Method

In this section, we will present our proposed method for classifying myopic maculopathy in detail. The architecture of our model is shown in Fig. 2. The model framework consists of four components: data augment, Swin-base, enhanced Arc-Face loss with 3 sub-centers, and weak label. Initially, in the supervised training phase, color fundus images are subjected to data augmentation, and the augmented images, along with their corresponding ground truth labels, are input to the Swin-base module for training, resulting in the initial Swin-MMC model. Then, in the semi-supervised training phase, the same model is applied once again to all fundus images to train the Swin-MMC model. Unlike other methods, we combined the training and validation sets to form a new image dataset by merging the true labels of the training data with those of the validation data to create the ground truth for the new dataset. This new dataset is used for three rounds of training, ultimately yielding the final Swin-MMC model. Throughout this process, the loss function employed is the En-ArcFace loss with 3 sub-centers.

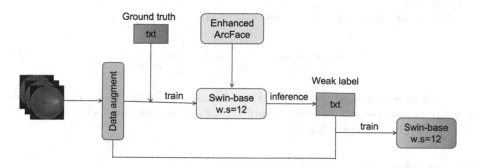

Fig. 2. The architecture of a Swin-MMC.

2.1 Enhanced ArcFace Loss with 3 Sub-centers

In the field of medical image processing, we applied the sub-center ArcFace loss function for the first time to calculate the loss. The enhanced ArcFace loss with 3 sub-centers is an improved version of the ArcFace loss, and it currently presents the best performance during the further test phase of MMAC Task 1. The En-ArcFace loss is widely used in face recognition tasks, capable of handling numerous facial categories [5]. This loss function can obtain more discriminative features compared to using softmax + cross-entropy because it calculates geodesic distance on a high-dimensional hypersphere, rather than Euclidean distance. Therefore, utilizing ArcFace loss as the loss function in the model enhances the ability to accurately discern variations among different lesion categories in fine-grained color fundus image classification tasks. This implies that the model is better equipped to accurately capture the differences between various lesion categories. Similar to many face recognition tasks, the myopic maculopathy classification task typically encompasses multiple categories. The En-ArcFace loss is specifically designed to handle a large number of categories and, after fine-tuning, proves to be well-suited for the task of myopic maculopathy classification. Our claims have also been validated through ablation experiments, as detailed in Table 5.

The most widely used softmax loss function for classification tasks is presented as follows:

$$L = -\log \frac{e^{W_{y_i}^T x_i + b_{y_i}}}{\sum_{j=1}^{N} e^{W_j^T x_i + b_j}}, \tag{1}$$

where $x_i \in R^d$ stands for the deep feature of the i-th sample, belonging to the y_i-th class, d stands for dimension. $W_j \in R^d$ the j-th column of the weight $W \in R^{d \times N}$. The number of classes in the classification task is N. $b_j \in R^N$ is the bias term. Then, by replacing $W_j^T x_i = \|W_j\| \|x_i\| \cos \theta_j$, We can now transform the logistic function into an ArcFace loss function, and s is the radius of the hypersphere.

The enhanced ArcFace loss [5] is presented as follows:

$$L' = -\log \frac{e^{s \cos(\theta_{y_i} + m)}}{e^{s \cos(\theta_{y_i} + m)} + \sum_{j=1, j \neq y_i}^{N} e^{s \cos \theta_j}}. \tag{2}$$

where θ_j is the angle between the weight W_j and the feature x_i. m is an additive angular margin penalty between x_i and W_{y_i}, $\theta_j = arccos\left(\max_k \left(W_{j_k}^T \mathbf{x}_i\right)\right), k \in \{1, \cdots, K\}$. In our paper, k is 3.

2.2   Weak Label

Weak Label Scheme Our weak label strategy includes the following steps:

- In the first stage, a special strategy different from the usual data augmentation methods was employed. Initially, the original training dataset and the validation dataset were merged into a new, larger dataset. The real labels of the original training data were combined with the real labels of the validation data to create the labels for the new dataset. Preprocessing of the dataset was carried out during this stage.
- In the second stage, the preprocessed fundus image data, along with the real labels, were input into the Swin-base model for training. This stage resulted in the initial Swin-MMC model and weak labels for the training dataset.

- In the third stage, the dataset obtained in the first stage was used as input images, and the weak labels generated in the second stage were used as input labels. They were input into the Swin-base model for further training.
- In the fourth stage, the operations from the second stage and third stages were repeated three times, ultimately leading to the final Swin-MMC model.

Advantages of Weak Label

- We create a larger dataset by merging the original training and validation data. This step aims to provide the model with a more diverse set of samples, enhancing its ability to learn image features and patterns effectively.
- Second, as depicted in Fig. 3, we employ the Swin-MMC model to transform the initial consistent labels into probability values representing each image's likelihood of belonging to different categories. These probability values are then used as training labels. The approach helps improve the model's generalization, enabling it to better handle noise and uncertainty in real-world applications.
- Furthermore, our weak label strategy involves a multi-stage training process, introducing more variations and diversity. This allows the model to better capture complex relationships and features within the data, thereby enhancing its robustness.
- Finally, the weak label strategy can be easily applied to other datasets and models.

In conclusion, the weak label strategy offers benefits such as dataset expansion, enhanced generalization, improved robustness, and adaptability to various datasets and models.

3   Experiments

3.1   Dataset and Evaluation Measures

In task 1 of the MMAC competition, the objective is to classify myopic maculopathy. The dataset for this task consists of a comprehensive collection of color

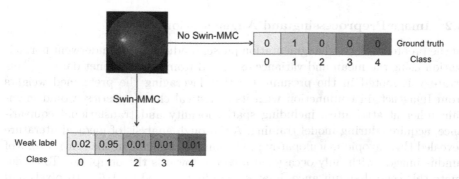

Fig. 3. The advantage of weak label.

fundus images. The training set comprises a total of 1143 images, sourced from two distinct data centers. Among these, 990 images originate from Data Center 1, while 153 images are obtained from Data Center 2. The validation set includes 248 color fundus images, with 215 images from Data Center 1 and an additional 33 images from Data Center 2. The test set contains 915 color fundus images, with 783 images originating from Data Center 1 and 132 images from Data Center 2. The detailed description of the data set is shown in Table 1.

Table 1. Data set descriptions.

Data set	Total images	Data center 1	Data center 2
Training set	1143	990 (87%)	153 (13%)
Validation set	248	215 (87%)	33 (13%)
Testing set	915	783 (86%)	132 (14%)

Furthermore, the dataset is enriched with essential patient metadata associated with each image, providing insights into age, sex, height (measured in centimeters, cm), and weight (measured in kilograms, kg). It is important to acknowledge the possibility of missing metadata values in some instances. This comprehensive dataset serves as the foundation for evaluating and advancing the performance of algorithms in the task of myopic maculopathy classification.

MMAC Task 1 aims to accurately determine whether a color fundus image falls into one of five categories: no macular lesions, tessellated fundus, diffuse chorioretinal atrophy, patchy chorioretinal atrophy, and macular atrophy. These categories are labeled with natural numbers: 0, 1, 2, 3, and 4, with higher numbers indicating more severe conditions. Consequently, the metrics calculation code utilizes quadratic weighted kappa (QWK), a widely employed evaluation metric for various medical imaging problems. QWK is a statistical measure designed to assess the agreement between two annotators. To ensure fairness, the evaluation metrics also include the F1 score and macro specificity, and individual metric scores are separately calculated on all test cases, and the final ranking score is obtained by averaging the scores of all metrics.

3.2   Image Preprocessing and Augmentation

In the preprocessing and augmentation phase, fundus images underwent normalization using the mean and variance extracted from the Imagenet dataset. This strategy is rooted in the presumption that leveraging the pretrained weights from Imagenet, in conjunction with its statistical characteristics, would maintain inherent attributes, including spatial locality and translational equivariance, acquired during model training. A thorough analysis of medical literature revealed that myopic maculopathy predominantly appears in the central zone of fundus images, with only occasional presence towards the periphery. To accentuate this central significance, images were first resized to 416×416 pixels and subsequently subjected to a central crop, yielding a resolution of 384×384 pixels to align with the model's input requirements. This procedure not only amplifies data heterogeneity but also minimizes peripheral noise. Given the standardized procedure of fundus image acquisition in clinical contexts, certain augmentations like vertical flipping or Gaussian blurring were considered redundant. Therefore, the only adopted augmentation was horizontal flipping, executed with a probability of 0.5, to preserve the diagnostic essence of the images.

3.3 Implementation Details

The configuration of our experimental setups, including the development environments and requirements, can be found in Table 2. Detailed procedures employed for training the Swin-MMC model are delineated in Table 3.

Table 2. Development environments and requirements.

Ubuntu version	Linux release
CUDA version	11.3
CPU	15 vCPU AMD EPYC 7543 32-Core
GPU (number and type)	1× NVIDIA A40 48GB Tensor Core GPU
Programming language	Python 3.8.0
Deep learning framework	Pytorch (Torch 1.11.0)
Specific dependencies	mmpretrain 1.0.0rc8
Code	https://github.com/LuliDreamAI/MICCAI_TASK1

In order to optimize model convergence and enrich the feature learning process during training, we incorporated a two-phase learning rate scheduling approach:

LinearLR Increasing Strategy. The initial learning rate is 0, and the strategy linearly increases the learning rate to 0.000125 for the first 5 epochs. After this period, the learning rate stabilizes, ensuring no further modifications. This method is predicated on the idea of hastening convergence in the nascent epochs by leveraging a relatively augmented learning rate.

CosineAnnealingLR Strategy. Commencing post the 5th epoch, this strategy employs a cosine annealing approach to the learning rate, setting a floor value at 1e-5. This progressive decrement of the learning rate, characterized by its cosine nature, facilitates intricate model tuning during the concluding training phases, steering the model to a more refined convergence point.

Table 3. Training protocols.

Basic network	Swin Transformer (base)
Network initialization	Pretrained weight in Imagenet1K and 21K
Batch size	32
Window size	12×12
Optimizer	Warmup with betas(0.9, 0.99)
Loss	Enhanced ArcFace loss with subcenter=3
Weight decay	0.05
Initial learning rate (lr)	0.000125
Training time per iteration	0.68 s

4   Results and Discussion

4.1   Results on Testing Set

In the testing set, the challenge uses several metrics, namely quadratic weighted kappa, macro F1, macro specificity, and average, for evaluation. It's important to note that the "average" metric is calculated as the mean value obtained from quadratic weighted kappa, macro F1, macro specificity, and specificity. In the testing phase, our method achieved second place with an average of 86.60%. In the further testing phase, it performed even better, improving by 1.63% and ultimately securing first place with an average surpassing the original first place by 0.71%. Detailed evaluation metric scores for our approach in both the testing phase and the further testing phase can be found in Table 4.

Table 4. The quantitative results of the test phase and further test phase.

Phase	Model	Volumetric(%) ↑			Average(%) ↑
		QWK	Macro F1	Macro Specificity	
Test	Swin-MMC	88.93	76.81	94.06	86.60
Further Test	Swin-MMC+Weak label	89.81	80.42	94.48	88.23

4.2   Visualization Heatmap Analysis

We input different original fundus images, as shown in Fig. 4(A), into the Swin-MMC model. The model generates a color fundus heatmap through the visualization layer, highlighting areas it deems most critical and displaying them using a color scale as depicted in Fig. 4(B). On the right side of Fig. 4, the cylinder corresponds to different colors as the numbers increase, indicating the regions that the model pays increasing attention to. We can observe that Swin-MMC is capable of learning and distinguishing the lesion areas of different categories of myopic maculopathy degeneration and correctly classifying the images into their respective.

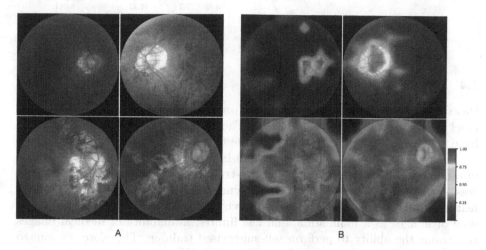

Fig. 4. Visualization of Swin-MMC for classifying the category of myopic maculopathy. **(A)** The different categories (Category 1 - Category 4) of myopic maculopathy in the original images. **(B)** Heatmaps generated on the deep features of the original images. Typical myopic maculopathy lesions were observed in hot regions.

4.3   Ablation Study in Further Test Phase

To validate the effectiveness of the En-ArcFace loss function and the weak label strategy in classifying Myopic Maculopathy, we conducted ablation experiments during the further test phase on both the Swin-MMC and Swin-MMC+Weak label models, as detailed in Table 5. For the Swin-MMC model, in the absence of the En-ArcFace loss function, the performance was at 87.04%. Introducing the En-ArcFace loss function improved the performance to 87.14%. Importantly, when incorporating the En-ArcFace loss function and combining it with the weak label strategy, the model's performance reached 88.23%. This represents a significant improvement of 1.63% compared to the previous 86.60% observed during the test phase. These results indicate that the En-ArcFace loss function and the weak label training strategy enable the model to capture the features of fundus images more accurately, thereby enhancing the overall model performance.

Table 5. Ablation experiments of En-ArcFace loss and weak label strategies.

Phase	Model	Loss		Volumetric(%) ↑			Average(%) ↑
		ArcFace	En-ArcFace	QWK	Macro F1	Macro Specificity	
Further Test	Swin-MMC	✓		89.87	77.04	94.22	87.04
			✓	89.88	77.24	94.32	87.14
	Swin-MMC+ Weak label	✓		**90.24**	79.67	94.41	88.11
			✓	89.81	**80.42**	**94.48**	**88.23**

4.4   Limitation and Future Work

Based on the Swin-base model, we have proposed a simple and effective weak label strategy, combined with the En-ArcFace loss function. Up to this point, we have achieved the best performance on the test data.

Moreover, we are confident that there is further potential for enhancement in our model. Firstly, self-supervised pre-training has achieved significant success in the field of image classification, enabling the learning of domain-level features from images. However, self-supervised pre-training requires a large volume of images as a foundation, and the limited availability of medical images constrains the ability to perform self-supervised training. Therefore, we aim to leverage weights pre-trained on ImageNet with self-supervised methods such as SimMIM [22] for continued training on fundus images, followed by fine-tuning with the pre-trained weights, which could yield promising results. Secondly, we can explore novel data augmentation techniques tailored to our retinal image dataset. Appropriate data augmentation strategies can enhance our performance when employing techniques like Test-Time Augmentation (TTA). Lastly, if there is no strict requirement for inference time, we may consider employing an ensemble approach with multiple models to enhance model performance.

5   Conclusion

In the classification of myopic maculopathy degeneration, our approach has successfully achieved high-precision recognition capability. There are two primary challenges facing this task: firstly, fundus images and general real-world images belong to different domains; secondly, the color representation of different diseases in the images is similar, making accurate classification particularly challenging.

To address these challenges, in comparison to other techniques, we innovatively proposed the use of En-ArcFace loss and weak label to improve the performance of our image classification algorithm. Specifically, the En-ArcFace loss provides a tighter feature embedding for classification tasks, aiding in distinguishing categories that look incredibly alike. Meanwhile, because the true label is too sharp, the weak label strategy offers an opportunity for the model to learn a more precise feature, further enhancing the model's generalization capability.

Through these methods, we have not only achieved outstanding results on the initial training dataset but also demonstrated superior performance on further test dataset, far surpassing traditional methods. This offers ophthalmologists a powerful tool to more accurately diagnose and differentiate types of myopic maculopathy degeneration, leading to more precise treatment recommendations for patients.

Acknowledgements. The authors of this paper declare that the classification method they implemented for participation in the MMAC 2023 challenge, targeting myopic maculopathy, utilized the Swin model trained on the publicly available and widely recognized dataset, ImageNet21k, and fine-tuned on the ImageNet1k dataset. The ImageNet21k dataset consists of approximately 14 million images and 21,000 classes, and the ImageNet1k dataset contains around 1,000,000 images across 1,000 categories. Moreover, no additional datasets other than those provided by the organizers were used. The proposed solution is fully automatic and devoid of any manual intervention. Lastly, this work was supported by the National Key Research and Development Program of China (No. 2022YFF0606303).

References

1. Almalik, F., Yaqub, M., Nandakumar, K.: Self-ensembling vision transformer (SEViT) for robust medical image classification. In: Wang, L., Dou, Q., Fletcher, P.T., Speidel, S., Li, S. (eds.) Medical Image Computing and Computer Assisted Intervention - MICCAI 2022. MICCAI 2022. LNCS, vol. 13433, pp. 376–386. Springer, Cham (2022). https://doi.org/10.1007/978-3-031-16437-8_36
2. Bilal, A., Zhu, L., Deng, A., Lu, H., Wu, N.: Ai-based automatic detection and classification of diabetic retinopathy using u-net and deep learning. Symmetry **14**(7), 1427 (2022)
3. Chen, R., et al.: Automatic recognition of ocular surface diseases on smartphone images using densely connected convolutional networks. In: 2021 43rd Annual International Conference of the IEEE Engineering in Medicine & Biology Society (EMBC), pp. 2786–2789. IEEE (2021)
4. Dai, L., et al.: A deep learning system for detecting diabetic retinopathy across the disease spectrum. Nat. Commun. **12**(1), 3242 (2021)
5. Deng, J., Guo, J., Xue, N., Zafeiriou, S.: ArcFace: additive angular margin loss for deep face recognition. In: Proceedings of the IEEE/CVF Conference on Computer Vision and Pattern Recognition, pp. 4690–4699 (2019)
6. Dosovitskiy, A., et al.: An image is worth 16x16 words: transformers for image recognition at scale. arXiv preprint arXiv:2010.11929 (2020)
7. Fang, Z., Xu, Z., He, X., Han, W.: Artificial intelligence-based pathologic myopia identification system in the ophthalmology residency training program. Front. Cell Dev. Biol. **10**, 1053079 (2022)
8. Gummadi, S.D., Ghosh, A.: Classification of ocular diseases: a vision transformer-based approach. In: Roy, S., Sinwar, D., Dey, N., Perumal, T., Tavares, J.M.R.S. (eds.) Innovations in Computational Intelligence and Computer Vision. ICICV 2022, LNNS, vol. 680, pp. 325–337. Springer, Singapore (2023). https://doi.org/10.1007/978-981-99-2602-2_25
9. Holden, B.A., et al.: Global prevalence of myopia and high myopia and temporal trends from 2000 through 2050. Ophthalmology **123**(5), 1036–1042 (2016)

10. Hossain, K.F., Kamran, S.A., Ong, J., Lee, A.G., Tavakkoli, A.: Revolutionizing space health (Swin-FSR): advancing super-resolution of fundus images for SANS visual assessment technology. In: Greenspan, H., et al. Medical Image Computing and Computer Assisted Intervention - MICCAI 2023, MICCAI 2023, LNCS, vol. 14226, pp 693–703. Springer, Cham (2023). https://doi.org/10.1007/978-3-031-43990-2_65

11. Khan, I.A., Sajeeb, A., Fattah, S.A.: An automatic ocular disease detection scheme from enhanced fundus images based on ensembling deep CNN networks. In: 2020 11th International Conference on Electrical and Computer Engineering (ICECE), pp. 491–494. IEEE (2020)

12. Liu, R., et al.: Deepdrid: diabetic retinopathy-grading and image quality estimation challenge. Patterns **3**(6), 100512 (2022)

13. Liu, Z., et al.: Swin transformer: Hierarchical vision transformer using shifted windows. In: Proceedings of the IEEE/CVF International Conference on Computer Vision, pp. 10012–10022 (2021)

14. Lu, L., et al.: Ai-model for identifying pathologic myopia based on deep learning algorithms of myopic maculopathy classification and "plus" lesion detection in fundus images. Front. Cell Dev. Biol. **9**, 719262 (2021)

15. Nawaz, M., et al.: An efficient deep learning approach to automatic glaucoma detection using optic disc and optic cup localization. Sensors **22**(2), 434 (2022)

16. Ohno-Matsui, K., et al.: International photographic classification and grading system for myopic maculopathy. Am. J. Ophthalmol. **159**(5), 877–883 (2015)

17. Potapenko, I., et al.: Automated artificial intelligence-based system for clinical follow-up of patients with age-related macular degeneration. Acta Ophthalmol. **100**(8), 927–936 (2022)

18. Sebastian, A., Elharrouss, O., Al-Maadeed, S., Almaadeed, N.: A survey on deep-learning-based diabetic retinopathy classification. Diagnostics **13**(3), 345 (2023)

19. Sun, Y., et al.: A deep network using coarse clinical prior for myopic maculopathy grading. Comput. Biol. Med. **154**, 106556 (2023)

20. Velpula, V.K., Sharma, L.D.: Multi-stage glaucoma classification using pre-trained convolutional neural networks and voting-based classifier fusion. Front. Physiol. **14**, 1–117588 (2023)

21. Wang, R., et al.: Efficacy of a deep learning system for screening myopic maculopathy based on color fundus photographs. Ophthalmol Therapy **12**(1), 469–484 (2023)

22. Xie, Z., et al.: Simmim: a simple framework for masked image modeling. In: Proceedings of the IEEE/CVF Conference on Computer Vision and Pattern Recognition, pp. 9653–9663 (2022)

23. Zang, P., Hormel, T.T., Hwang, T.S., Bailey, S.T., Huang, D., Jia, Y.: Deep-learning-aided diagnosis of diabetic retinopathy, age-related macular degeneration, and glaucoma based on structural and angiographic oct. Ophthalmol. Sci. **3**(1), 100245 (2023)

Towards Label-Efficient Deep Learning for Myopic Maculopathy Classification

Junlin Hou[1], Jilan Xu[1], Fan Xiao[2], Bo Zhang[2], Yiqian Xu[1], Yuejie Zhang[1], Haidong Zou[3], and Rui Feng[1,2(✉)]

[1] School of Computer Science, Shanghai Key Laboratory of Intelligent Information Processing, Fudan University, Shanghai, China
{jlhou18,fengrui}@fudan.edu.cn
[2] Academy for Engineering and Technology, Fudan University, Shanghai, China
[3] Department of Ophthalmology, Shanghai General Hospital, School of Medicine, Shanghai Jiao Tong University, Shanghai, China

Abstract. Myopic Maculopathy is the leading cause of legal blindness in patients with pathologic myopia. Automated myopic maculopathy diagnosis is of vital importance to early treatment and progression slowdown. However, the scarcity of labeled fundus images with myopic maculopathy makes it challenging to improve diagnostic performance via deep learning models. In this paper, we construct a label-efficient deep learning framework for myopic maculopathy classification. In specific, we exploit two categories of pre-training methods, i.e., vision-language pre-training and self-supervised visual representation learning, to alleviate the overfitting problem caused by the limited number of training images. Moreover, we adopt a semi-supervised learning technique, namely pseudo labeling, to leverage a large number of unlabeled fundus images from external datasets. We also investigate the impact of other key components in model training for better performance, including backbone architecture, input resolution, and loss function. Our method is evaluated in the MICCAI 2023 Myopic Maculopathy Analysis Challenge (MMAC). Among 17 participating teams, our ensembled model *ranked 1st* on the leaderboard with an average score of 0.8752. The code will be publicly available at https://github.com/FDU-VTS/MMAC.

Keywords: Myopic Maculopathy · Label-efficient · Vision-language Pre-training · Self-supervised Learning · Semi-supervised Learning

1 Introduction

Myopic maculopathy has become one of the major causes of legal blindness and visual impairment in patients with pathologic myopia worldwide [19]. According

This work was supported by the National Natural Science Foundation of China (No. 62172101), Chinese National Key Research and Development Program (No. 2021YFC2702100), the Science and Technology Commission of Shanghai Municipality (No. 21511104502).

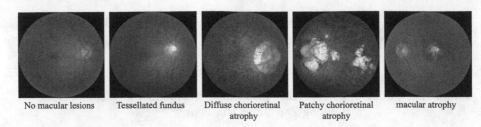

| No macular lesions | Tessellated fundus | Diffuse chorioretinal atrophy | Patchy chorioretinal atrophy | macular atrophy |

Fig. 1. Examples from MMAC dataset of different categories, including no macular lesions, tessellated fundus, diffuse chorioretinal atrophy, patchy chorioretinal atrophy, and macular atrophy.

to the ATN classification system [21], the severity of myopic maculopathy can be divided into five categories, including no macular lesions, tessellated fundus, diffuse chorioretinal atrophy, patchy chorioretinal atrophy, and macular atrophy. Each severity grade is determined by the presence of the chorioretinal atrophy, which may appear in different patterns. Considering the irreversible visual disability caused by myopic maculopathy, routine screening and early treatment are important to the disease control.

In recent years, deep learning approaches have achieved promising performance in various ophthalmic disease diagnosis on fundus images, especially diabetic retinopathy (DR) [6,9,18], age-related macular degeneration (AMD) [1], and glaucoma [5]. In comparison, the research on automated myopic maculopathy is still largely unexplored. All the previous works [22,24] were conducted on their private datasets. Current challenges lie in the lack of sufficient publicly available data.

In this work, we propose label-efficient deep learning approaches for the classification of myopic maculopathy on fundus images. Our methods are demonstrated effective in the MICCAI 2023 Myopic Maculopathy Analysis Challenge (MMAC)[1]. It is the first public dataset that covers the classification and segmentation of myopic maculopathy, and the prediction of spherical equivalent, with fundus images. This dataset largely catalyzes future research on automated myopic maculopathy analysis in the research community. Figure 1 illustrates some examples from the classification of myopic maculopathy subset with different severity grades. In our solution, we develop two popular label-efficient deep learning methods to alleviate the overfitting problem caused by the limited amount of data. First, we finetune several advanced models pre-trained by vision-language pre-training on medical image-text pairs or self-supervised learning on large-scale fundus images. Second, we perform pseudo labeling, a semi-supervised learning technique, to leverage a large number of unlabeled fundus images iteratively. Moreover, we comprehensively analyze the impact of several key components in model development, including network architecture, input image resolution, and loss function. Finally, multiple models are ensembled to

---

[1] https://codalab.lisn.upsaclay.fr/competitions/12441

further improve the model's generalization ability. Extensive experiments on MMAC dataset show that our proposed solutions achieve superior performance for myopic maculopathy classification, ranking 1st on the challenge leaderboard.

2 Related Work

Deep learning approaches have demonstrated significant improvement in diagnosing various ophthalmic diseases on fundus images. For diabetic retinopathy (DR), Dai et al. [3] proposed a deep learning system, named DeepDR, for multiple purposes including real-time image quality assessment, lesion detection and DR grading. Hou et al. [10] proposed a Cross-field Transformer to exploit the correlation of two-field fundus images for DR screening. Xue et al. [25] designed deep learning-based networks for the diagnosis of DR with cataracts based on infrared fundus images. For glaucoma, Fu et al. [5] proposed a disc-aware ensemble network based on global fundus image and local optic disc region for glaucoma screening. Zhao et al. [28] proposed a weakly-supervised multi-task learning method to jointly perform evidence identification, optic disc segmentation, and glaucoma diagnosis. For age-related macular degeneration (AMD), Burlina et al. [1] studied the appropriateness of utilizing image features extracted from pre-trained deep neural networks for the AMD detection task.

Compared to the above-mentioned common ophthalmic diseases, the research on automated classification of myopic maculopathy via deep learning methods still remains largely unexplored. Wang et al. [24] developed a deep learning system based on EfficientNet-b8 for detection and classification of myopic maculopathy. Sun et al. [22] proposed a myopic maculopathy grading framework, comprised of a prior knowledge extraction module and a feature fusion module. The successful experiences in diagnosing other ophthalmic diseases can be readily applied to myopic maculopathy. However, the current challenges primarily stem from the scarcity of publicly available data. Therefore, it is crucial to investigate label-efficient deep learning methods to improve diagnostic accuracy under limited training samples.

3 Methodology

As depicted in Fig. 2, the overall architecture of our model consists of three stages, i.e., hybrid pre-training, domain-specific finetuning, and semi-supervised learning. Specifically, to alleviate the overfitting problem caused by limited samples, we adopt two label-efficient learning approaches. One is pre-training where vision-language pre-training and self-supervised visual representation learning are fully exploited. The other is pseudo-labeling, a semi-supervised method which leverages both labeled and unlabeled data. Besides, we also investigate different key components in deep networks, including backbone architecture, image resolution, loss function, and model ensemble.

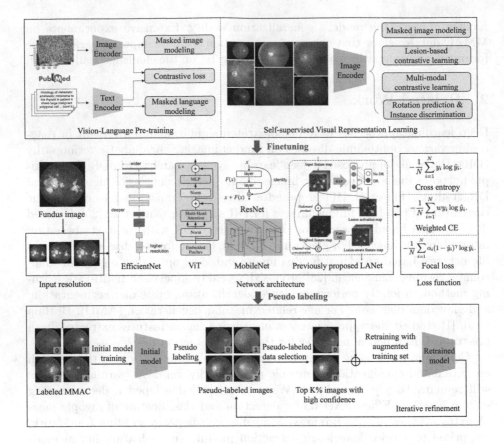

Fig. 2. An overall structure of our proposed label-efficient deep learning framework for the classification of myopic maculopathy.

3.1 Pre-training

Considering the limited amount of data, we leverage several pre-trained models and finetune on the MMAC dataset to avoid the overfitting problem and further improve the model's generalization ability. We divide these pre-training methods into two categories, i.e, vision-language pre-training and self-supervised learning.

Vision-Language Pre-training. Vision-language pre-training (VLP) refers to training deep learning models on large-scale multi-modal datasets containing paired visual and textual data. We extract the vision encoder from medical VLP frameworks and finetune it on the downstream myopic maculopathy classification task. (1) BiomedCLIP [27] adapts CLIP [20] for the biomedical domain, using PMC-15M dataset with 15 million figure-caption pairs extracted from biomedical research articles in PubMed Central. (2) BiomedGPT [26] employs prevalent unimodal strategies, including masked language modeling and masked image infilling, and multi-modal techniques, such as visual question answering and captioning during the pre-training phase on 14 medical datasets. (3) PMC-CLIP [17] constructs a CLIP-style model with image-text contrastive loss and masked language modeling loss on PMC-OA, a biomedical dataset with 1.6M image-caption pairs collected from PubMedCentral's OpenAccess subset.

Self-supervised Learning. Self-supervised learning (SSL) aims to learn feature representations by a pretext task, where the labels are generated from inherent structure or information present in the image itself automatically. We leverage the self-supervised learning models pre-trained on fundus images. (1) A lesion-based contrastive learning method [12] based on ResNet50 takes lesion patches as the input to learn representations that are highly discriminative for retinal disease diagnosis. (2) Uni4Eye [2] is a universal self-supervised framework, which builds its basis on a masked image modeling task with a ViT architecture on 2D and 3D ophthalmic images. (3) A self-supervised learning method [15] exploits multi-modal data (i.e., color fundus photography and fundus fluorescein angiography) to learn modality-invariant features and patient-similarity features for more accurate diagnosis. (4) A rotation-oriented collaborative method [14] is proposed to explore rotation-related and rotation-invariant features in self-supervised pre-training to capture discriminative structures from fundus images.

3.2   Network Architecture

In this work, we explore the impact of different advanced deep learning network architectures for myopic maculopathy classification, including various popular backbone networks [4,7,11,23] and our previously proposed lesion-aware network [8].

Popular Backbone Networks. (1) ResNet [7] is one of the most widely-used networks in various computer vision tasks. It introduces residual structures and leverages identity mappings to address the network degradation problem. (2) To leverage the advantages of the network's depth, width, and resolution, Efficient-Net [23] presents a more generalized perspective on optimizing deep learning networks by introducing a simple and efficient compound scaling method. EfficientNet maintains a good trade-off between model size and accuracy. (3) Vision Transformer (ViT) [4] takes a sequence of tokenized image patches as input into a Transformer encoder, which consists of alternating layers of multi-head attention and MLP blocks. By encoding both spatial and positional information, ViT is capable of modeling long-range dependencies and effectively capturing global context within an image. (4) As a lightweight network, MobileNet [11] adopts depthwise separable convolutions as its fundamental building blocks. By decomposing convolutions into depthwise convolutions and pointwise convolutions, MobileNet has fewer parameters and ensures higher efficiency.

Previously Proposed Lesion-Aware Network. In our previous work [8], we propose a weakly-supervised lesion-aware network (LANet) for diabetic retinopathy (DR) grading, which enhances the discriminative features with lesion priors by only image-level supervision. LANet contains a lesion attention module that generates lesion activation maps by introducing an auxiliary DR identification task. Lesion activation maps are utilized to assist the network to focus on the most relevant regions for boosting performance. Besides, an adaptive joint loss is designed to balance the identification and grading tasks dynamically. Apart from DR grading, LANet can be easily transferred to the diagnosis of other fundus diseases. In this work, we adopt LANet for the classification of myopic maculopathy.

3.3   Pseudo Labeling

Pseudo labeling is a simple yet effective approach used in semi-supervised learning. Apart from the labeled MMAC dataset, other public datasets of fundus images are easy to acquire and be regarded as unlabeled data. By leveraging labeled data and a large amount of unlabeled data, pseudo labeling aims to enhance the model's generalization and performance on the myopic maculopathy classification task. In this work, the process of pseudo labeling involves the following steps, as shown in the bottom row of Fig. 2.

- Initial Model Training: The model is initially trained on the MMAC dataset via supervised learning. This trained model serves as the starting point for pseudo labeling.
- Pseudo Labeling: The fundus images from other public datasets are regarded as unlabeled data and fed into the trained model, and the model's predictions are used to assign pseudo labels to these unlabeled samples.
- Pseudo-labeled Data Selection: Since the generated pseudo label might be noisy or incorrect, for a given image, the pseudo-label is only retained if the model produces a high-confidence prediction. This can be achieved by selecting the top $K\%$ samples whose pseudo labels are of high class probability.
- Retraining with Augmented Training Set: The labeled data and the newly pseudo-labeled data are combined to create an augmented training set. The model is retrained using the augmented training set.
- Iterative Refinement: The process of pseudo labeling and retraining is repeated iteratively.

Algorithm 1 summarizes our pseudo labeling approach for myopic maculopathy classification.

Algorithm 1. Pseudo labeling

Input: Labeled dataset $D_L = \{x_L^i, y_L^i\}_{i=1}^N$ with N samples, Unlabeled dataset $D_U = \{x_U^i\}_{i=1}^M$ with M samples, Batch size B, Classification model $F_\theta(\cdot)$, Training epochs E, Learning rate γ, Total classes C, Total iterations of pseudo labeling T, Selection ratio K.

1: **for** $t \in \{1, \ldots, T\}$ **do**
2:      **for** $e \in \{1, \ldots, E\}$ **do**
3:          **for** sampled minibatch $\{x_L^i\}_{i=1}^{B}$ **do**
4:              $\mathcal{L}_{ce} = -\frac{1}{B} \sum_{i=1}^{B} y_L^i \log F_\theta(x_L^i)$
5:              $\theta' = \theta - \gamma \nabla F_\theta(x_L)$
6:          **end for**
7:      **end for**
8:      **for** $i \in \{1, \ldots, M\}$ **do**
9:          Calculate class probability $p_U^i = F_{\theta'}(x_U^i)$.
10:         Generate pseudo label $\hat{y}_U^i = \arg\max_c p_U^i(c)$
11:      **end for**
12:      Sort $D_U = \{x_U^i, \hat{y}_U^i, p_U^i\}_{i=1}^{M}$ based on predicted class logit $p_U^i(\hat{y}_U^i)$.
13:      Select Top-$K(\%)$ samples to form pseudo-labeled subset $D_P = \{x_U^i, \hat{y}_U^i\}_{i=1}^{MK}$.
14:      $D_L = D_L \cup D_P$
15: **end for**
16: **return** Classification network $F_{\theta'}(\cdot)$

3.4   Image Resolution

The resolution of fundus images plays a crucial role in myopic maculopathy classification. Higher input resolution enables capturing subtle pathological changes, allowing for more accurate identification and characterization of abnormalities. In this work, we investigate different input resolutions from 128×128 to 600×600 to determine a sufficient input size for maximizing the diagnostic performance.

3.5   Loss Function

The loss function is a fundamental component in deep learning models. Let $D = \{(x_i, y_i)\}_{i=1}^{N}$ denotes the training set with N samples, where x_i is the input image and y_i is the corresponding ground truth label. We explore three different loss functions to quantify the discrepancy between predicted outputs $\hat{y}_i$ and one-hot ground truth labels y.

Cross-Entropy Loss. The cross-entropy loss is a widely used loss function in classification tasks, which can be calculated as:

$$\mathcal{L}_{ce}(y, \hat{y}) = -\frac{1}{N} \sum_{i=1}^{N} y_i \log \hat{y}_i. \tag{1}$$

Weighted Cross-Entropy Loss. The weighted cross-entropy loss is a variant of the standard cross-entropy loss that addresses the issue of class imbalance. It assigns different weights to the classes based on their importance or prevalence. Given the pre-defined weight of each class $w = [w_0, ..., w_{C-1}]$, where C denotes the number of class, the weighted cross-entropy loss can be expressed as:

$$\mathcal{L}_{wce}(y, \hat{y}) = -\frac{1}{N} \sum_{i=1}^{N} w y_i \log \hat{y}_i. \tag{2}$$

Focal Loss. The focal loss [16] is a loss function specifically designed to address the challenges of class imbalance and hard samples in classification tasks. It introduces a modulating factor into cross-entropy to assign higher weights to misclassified samples and gradually reduce the weight for well-classified samples, which can be defined as:

$$\mathcal{L}_{fl}(y, \hat{y}) = -\frac{1}{N} \sum_{i=1}^{N} \alpha_i (1 - \hat{y}_i)^\gamma \log \hat{y}_i, \tag{3}$$

where α_i is a balancing factor and γ is a focusing parameter.

3.6   Model Ensemble

Model ensemble is an useful technique that involves combining the predictions of multiple individual models to improve overall performance and generalization. Various ensemble strategies include voting, bagging, boosting, and stacking. In our work, we obtain the final prediction of each fundus image by averaging the predictions from individual models.

4   Experiment

4.1   Dataset

The MMAC dataset for the classification of myopic maculopathy contains five grades, i.e. no macular lesions, tessellated fundus, diffuse chorioretinal atrophy, patchy chorioretinal atrophy and macular atrophy. Training set consists of 1143 color fundus images, with 990 images from Data Center 1 and 153 images from Data Center 2. Validation set contains 248 color fundus images, with 215 images from Data Center 1 and 33 images from Data Center 2. Testing set consists of 915 color fundus images, with 783 images from Data Center 1 and 132 images from Data Center 2, and the labels are not available during the challenge.

4.2 Implementation Details

In the training phase, we adopt strong data augmentation, including random cropping, flipping, rotation, color jittering, gaussian blur, gray scale, and sharpness. We train the networks for 100 epochs with a batch size of 32 using the Adam optimizer. The initial learning rate is set to 1e-4, and decay by cosine annealing learning rate schedule. The methods were implemented on the PyTorch platform and run on Tesla V100 GPUs.

Table 1. Results of different pre-trained models on the validation set.

ID	Pre-train	Method	Backbone	Resolution	Dataset	Avg score
0	VLP	BiomedCLIP [27]	ViT_{base}	224×224	PMC-15M	0.7838
1		BiomedGPT$_{small}$ [26]	ResNet50	256×256	14 datasets	0.8008
2		PMC-CLIP [17]	ResNet50	512×512	PMC-OA	0.8107
3	SSL	Lesion-based CL [12]	ResNet50	512×512	EyePACS	0.8131
4		Uni4eye [2]	ViT_{large}	224×224	mmOphth-v1	0.8157
5		Multi-modal SSL [15]	ResNet18	512×512	Fundus-FFA	0.8440
6		Rotation-oriented [14]	ResNet18	512×512	EyePACS	0.8445

Table 2. Results of different backbone architectures on the validation set.

Backbone	ID	Baseline	ID	LANet
ResNet18 [7]	7	0.8047	13	0.8261
ResNet50 [7]	8	0.7908	14	0.8378
Mobilev3 [11]	9	0.8392	15	0.8589
EfficientNet-b0 [23]	10	0.8448	16	0.8411
EfficientNet-b1 [23]	11	0.8795	17	0.8786
EfficientNet-b2 [23]	12	0.8413	18	0.8590

Table 3. Results of different input resolutions on the validation set.

ID	Resolution	FLOPs	Avg score
19	128×128	0.199G	0.8131
20	224×224	0.609G	0.8413
21	384×384	1.789G	0.8658
22	448×448	2.434G	0.8723
23	512×512	3.179G	0.8795
24	600×600	6.520G	0.8778

4.3 Evaluation Metrics

To evaluate the classification performance of the proposed methods, we follow the challenge protocols and adopt quadratic-weighted kappa, F1 score and specificity as evaluation metrics. The ranking score is obtained by averaging the scores of all the three metrics.

4.4 Results on the Validation Set

Analysis on Pre-trained Model. We adopt several advanced pre-trained models via vision-language pre-training and self-supervised learning for our myopic maculopathy classification task, and the results are shown in Table 1. In general, the group of SSL models outperform VLP models. The reason is that these SSL models are pre-trained on fundus image datasets, so that the learned representations of fundus structure might benefit our downstream task. In contrast, VLP models are pre-trained on a large variety of medical image modalities and text descriptions, lacking of the specificity on fundus image domain. Among SSL models, Lesion-based CL with ResNet50 and Uni4eye with ViT_{large} backbones might cause overfitting problems on the downstream task with small number of samples and lead to inferior performance. In contrast, Multi-modal SSL and Rotation-oriented methods with lighter backbone (ResNet18) show higher performance of over 0.84 val score.

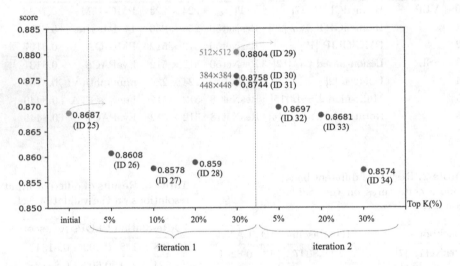

Fig. 3. Results of pseudo labeling under different selection ratio K in two iterations.

Analysis on Backbone Architecture. First, we evaluate the effects of several popular backbone networks, including ResNet [7], MobileNet [11], and Efficient-Net [23]. As can be seen from Table 2, ResNet models achieve inferior diagnostic performance of around 0.80 average score, while the light-weighted MobileNetv3 model obtains a superior result of 0.8392 average score. All EfficientNet models outperform the above models with a large margin, where EfficientNet-b1 reaches the best performance on the validation set with 0.8795 score. The results fully demonstrate the superiority of EfficientNet.

Then, we investigate our previously proposed lesion-aware network (LANet) based on these backbone architectures. As illustrated in Table 2, incorporating the lesion attention module shows superior or comparable performance on all the backbones. In particular, LANet presents significant improvements by 4.7%

on ResNet50, 2.1% on ResNet18, 1.9% on Mobilev3, and 1.8% on EfficientNet-b2. The results verify the effectiveness and generality of the proposed LANet on different backbones.

Analysis on Pseudo Labeling. We next evaluate the effect of pseudo labeling algorithm. A large number of fundus images from DDR dataset [13] are collected as unlabeled data. As shown in Fig. 3, after training the initial EfficientNet-b1 model, we perform two iterations of pseudo labeling under different selection ratio K. The models marked as red points are utilized to generate pseudo labels for the next iteration. In iteration 1, selecting the top 30% pseudo-labeled images with high class probabilities achieves a significant improvement, leading to the best-performed single model with 0.8804 average score among all the other models in this work. We also train the models with different input resolution under this setting. In iteration 2, the performance remains stable and does not show an obvious improvement.

Analysis on Input Resolution. We also study the influence of different input resolutions based on EfficientNet-b1 architecture. As shown in Table 3, myopic maculopathy classification benefits from larger input resolutions at the cost of higher computational expenses. We can observe a significant improvement from 128×128 to 384×384 and a stable performance between 384×384 and 600×600. Considering the trade-off between performance and computational cost, the 512×512 input resolution is adopted in our experiments.

Table 4. Results of different loss functions on the validation set.

Loss function	Parameter setting	Average score			
		ID	EfficientNet-b1	ID	Rotation-oriented
Cross Entropy (CE)	–	35	0.8795	40	0.8445
Weighted CE	[0.05, 0.05, 0.09, 0.34, 0.47]	36	0.8510	–	–
Weighted CE	[1., 1., 1., 1., 2.]	37	0.8793	41	0.8464
Weighted CE	[1., 1., 1., 1., 5.]	38	0.8788	42	0.8562
Focal [16]	$\gamma = 2$	39	0.8730	43	0.8601

Analysis on Loss Function. Finally, we evaluate three loss functions using EfficientNet-b1 and Rotation-oriented ResNet18. For the weighted CE loss, we pre-define three weights for each class. The first group [0.05, 0.05, 0.09, 0.34, 0.47] is calculated by the inverse of the percentage of the class samples in the training set. The other two groups assign larger weights (2 and 5) on the fifth class of macular atrophy, which contains less samples, and remain the rest classes' weights as 1. For the focal loss, γ is set to be 2. Results from Table 4 illustrate that the weighted CE with class-balanced weights achieves poor performance.

A plausible reason is that the imbalanced class distribution of the training set is consistent with that of the validation set. The other loss functions achieve comparable performance.

4.5 Results on the MMAC Leaderboard

Submitted Results. In the testing phase, we ensemble multiple models to further boost the performance of myopic maculopathy classification. The final prediction of each fundus image is obtained by averaging the predictions from individual models. We submit four combinations of ensemble models for the testing dataset of MMAC challenge. As can be seen from Table 5, with the increased number of ensemble models, the diagnostic performance continues to improve. Our final ensemble model composed of 24 models reaches the best results on all the evaluation metrics.

Table 5. Results of the ensemble models on the test set.

ID	Ensemble model ID	#Model	Kappa	Macro F1	Specificity	Average score
44	21,22,23,37,38,39,29,30,31,5,6	11	0.8958	0.7644	0.9438	0.8680
45	44,36,26,27,28,32,33,17	18	0.8949	0.7644	0.9424	0.8672
46	44,41,42,43,14,17,32,33	18	0.8966	0.7732	0.9434	0.8711
47	44,36,26,27,28,17,32, 33,41,42,43,14,12,34	24	0.9005	0.7807	0.9445	0.8752

Table 6. Top-10 results on the MMAC challenge leaderboard.

Rank	Team name	Kappa	Macro F1	Specificity	Average score
1	**fdvts_mm (ours)**	**0.9005 (1)**	**0.7807 (1)**	**0.9445 (1)**	**0.8752 (1)**
2	DGUT_luli	0.8893 (5)	0.7681 (2)	0.9406 (6)	0.8660 (2)
3	Taco Friday	0.8995 (2)	0.7513 (4)	0.9407 (5)	0.8638 (3)
4	hyeonminkim0625	0.8928 (4)	0.7528 (3)	0.9409 (4)	0.8622 (4)
5	AIFuture	0.8951 (3)	0.7360 (5)	0.9422 (3)	0.8578 (5)
6	fyii200	0.8786 (8)	0.7229 (8)	0.9424 (2)	0.8479 (6)
7	suibe_qt	0.8812 (7)	0.7244 (7)	0.9367 (8)	0.8474 (7)
8	latim	0.8858 (6)	0.7081 (9)	0.9396 (7)	0.8445 (8)
9	micolab	0.8707 (9)	0.7289 (6)	0.9336 (11)	0.8444 (9)
10	THU_HIT_SZCoops	0.8659 (10)	0.6748 (10)	0.9314 (12)	0.8240 (10)

Results on the Leaderboard. Table 6 shows the Top-10 results on the MMAC challenge leaderboard. Our ensemble model ranks 1st on both the overall and individual evaluation metrics. Our model achieves 0.9005 on Kappa, 0.7807 on Macro F1, 0.9445 on Specificity, surpassing the second team by near 1% on Average score. The result indicates that our model shows better diagnostic performance and generalization ability for myopic maculopathy classification task.

5   Conclusion

In this work, we propose a label-efficient deep learning framework for automated classification of myopic maculopathy. We particularly adopt pre-trained models via vision-language pre-training or self-supervised visual representation learning, which serve as useful substrates for the downstream myopic maculopathy classification task. We also employ the pseudo labeling technique to leverage a large amount of unlabeled data effectively. Moreover, we investigate some important components in improving model performance, where backbone architecture has the most significant impact. On the MMAC challenge learderboard, our ensembled model ranked 1st among all the participating teams.

References

1. Burlina, P., Freund, D.E., Joshi, N., Wolfson, Y., Bressler, N.M.: Detection of age-related macular degeneration via deep learning. In: 2016 IEEE 13th International Symposium on Biomedical Imaging (ISBI), pp. 184–188. IEEE (2016)
2. Cai, Z., Lin, L., He, H., Tang, X.: Uni4Eye: unified 2d and 3d self-supervised pre-training via masked image modeling transformer for ophthalmic image classification. In: Wang, L., Dou, Q., Fletcher, P.T., Speidel, S., Li, S. (eds.) Medical Image Computing and Computer Assisted Intervention - MICCAI 2022. MICCAI 2022, LNCS, vol. 13438, pp. 88–98. Springer, Cham (2022). https://doi.org/10.1007/978-3-031-16452-1_9
3. Dai, L., et al.: A deep learning system for detecting diabetic retinopathy across the disease spectrum. Nat. Commun. **12**(1), 3242 (2021)
4. Dosovitskiy, A., et al.: An image is worth 16×16 words: transformers for image recognition at scale. arXiv preprint arXiv:2010.11929 (2020)
5. Fu, H., et al.: Disc-aware ensemble network for glaucoma screening from fundus image. IEEE Trans. Med. Imaging **37**(11), 2493–2501 (2018)
6. Gulshan, V., et al.: Development and validation of a deep learning algorithm for detection of diabetic retinopathy in retinal fundus photographs. Jama **316**(22), 2402–2410 (2016)
7. He, K., Zhang, X., Ren, S., Sun, J.: Deep residual learning for image recognition. In: Proceedings of the IEEE Conference on Computer Vision and Pattern Recognition, pp. 770–778 (2016)
8. Hou, J., et al.: Diabetic retinopathy grading with weakly-supervised lesion priors. In: ICASSP 2023–2023 IEEE International Conference on Acoustics, Speech and Signal Processing (ICASSP), pp. 1–5. IEEE (2023)

9. Hou, J., Xiao, F., Xu, J., Zhang, Y., Zou, H., Feng, R.: Deep-OCTA: ensemble deep learning approaches for diabetic retinopathy analysis on OCTA images. In: Sheng, B., Aubreville, M. (eds.) Mitosis Domain Generalization and Diabetic Retinopathy Analysis. MIDOG DRAC 2022 2022. LNCS, vol. 13597, pp. 74–87. Springer, Cham (2023). https://doi.org/10.1007/978-3-031-33658-4_8

10. Hou, J., et al.: Cross-field transformer for diabetic retinopathy grading on two-field fundus images. In: 2022 IEEE International Conference on Bioinformatics and Biomedicine (BIBM), pp. 985–990. IEEE (2022)

11. Howard, A.G., et al.: Mobilenets: efficient convolutional neural networks for mobile vision applications. arXiv preprint arXiv:1704.04861 (2017)

12. Huang, Y., Lin, L., Cheng, P., Lyu, J., Tang, X.: Lesion-based contrastive learning for diabetic retinopathy grading from fundus images. In: de Bruijne, M., et al. Medical Image Computing and Computer Assisted Intervention - MICCAI 2021, MICCAI 2021, LNCS, Part II, vol. 12902, pp. 113–123. Springer, Cham (2021). https://doi.org/10.1007/978-3-030-87196-3_11

13. Li, T., Gao, Y., Wang, K., Guo, S., Liu, H., Kang, H.: Diagnostic assessment of deep learning algorithms for diabetic retinopathy screening. Inf. Sci. **501**, 511–522 (2019)

14. Li, X., et al.: Rotation-oriented collaborative self-supervised learning for retinal disease diagnosis. IEEE Trans. Med. Imaging **40**(9), 2284–2294 (2021)

15. Li, X., Jia, M., Islam, M.T., Yu, L., Xing, L.: Self-supervised feature learning via exploiting multi-modal data for retinal disease diagnosis. IEEE Trans. Med. Imaging **39**(12), 4023–4033 (2020)

16. Lin, T.Y., Goyal, P., Girshick, R., He, K., Dollár, P.: Focal loss for dense object detection. In: Proceedings of the IEEE International Conference on Computer Vision, pp. 2980–2988 (2017)

17. Lin, W., et al.: Pmc-clip: contrastive language-image pre-training using biomedical documents. arXiv preprint arXiv:2303.07240 (2023)

18. Liu, R., et al.: DeepDRiD: diabetic retinopathy-grading and image quality estimation challenge. Patterns **3**(6), 100512 (2022)

19. Ohno-Matsui, K., et al.: International photographic classification and grading system for myopic maculopathy. Am. J. Ophthalmol. **159**(5), 877–883 (2015)

20. Radford, A., et al.: Learning transferable visual models from natural language supervision. In: International Conference on Machine Learning, pp. 8748–8763. PMLR (2021)

21. Ruiz-Medrano, J., Montero, J.A., Flores-Moreno, I., Arias, L., García-Layana, A., Ruiz-Moreno, J.M.: Myopic maculopathy: current status and proposal for a new classification and grading system (ATN). Prog. Retin. Eye Res. **69**, 80–115 (2019)

22. Sun, Y., Li, Y., Zhang, F., Zhao, H., Liu, H., Wang, N., Li, H.: A deep network using coarse clinical prior for myopic maculopathy grading. Comput. Biol. Med. **154**, 106556 (2023)

23. Tan, M., Le, Q.: EfficientNet: rethinking model scaling for convolutional neural networks. In: International Conference on Machine Learning, pp. 6105–6114. PMLR (2019)

24. Wang, R., et al.: Efficacy of a deep learning system for screening myopic maculopathy based on color fundus photographs. Ophthalmol Ther. **12**(1), 469–484 (2023)

25. Xue, W., et al.: Deep learning-based analysis of infrared fundus photography for automated diagnosis of diabetic retinopathy with cataracts. J. Cataract Refract. Surg. **49**(10), 1043–1048 (2023)

26. Zhang, K., et al.: BiomedGPT: a unified and generalist biomedical generative pre-trained transformer for vision, language, and multimodal tasks. arXiv preprint arXiv:2305.17100 (2023)
27. Zhang, S., et al.: Large-scale domain-specific pretraining for biomedical vision-language processing. arXiv preprint arXiv:2303.00915 (2023)
28. Zhao, R., Liao, W., Zou, B., Chen, Z., Li, S.: Weakly-supervised simultaneous evidence identification and segmentation for automated glaucoma diagnosis. In: Proceedings of the AAAI Conference on Artificial Intelligence, vol. 33, pp. 809–816 (2019)

Ensemble Deep Learning Approaches for Myopic Maculopathy Plus Lesions Segmentation

Fan Xiao[1], Junlin Hou[2], Jilan Xu[2], Yiqian Xu[2], Bo Zhang[1], Yuejie Zhang[2], Haidong Zou[3], and Rui Feng[1,2(✉)]

[1] Academy for Engineering and Technology, Fudan University, Shanghai, China
`21210860085@m.fudan.edu.cn`, `19110860073@fudan.edu.cn`
[2] School of Computer Science, Shanghai Key Laboratory of Intelligent Information Processing, Fudan University, Shanghai, China
`{jlhou18,jilanxu18,xuyiqian,yjzhang,fengrui}@fudan.edu.cn`
[3] Department of Ophthalmology, Shanghai General Hospital, School of Medicine, Shanghai Jiao Tong University, Shanghai, China
`zouhaidong@sjtu.edu.cn`

Abstract. Myopia is a leading cause of visual impairment and blindness in several countries. Effective diagnosis and intervention are crucial, typically relying on manual image analysis by ophthalmologists, which is time-consuming and experience-dependent. In this work, we introduce an ensemble of deep learning techniques for myopic maculopathy plus lesions segmentation. Specifically, we utilize UNet, UNet++, and DeeplabV3+ to segment three lesions with strong data augmentation. Our ensembled model has proved to be effective in the MICCAI 2023 Myopic Maculopathy Analysis Challenge (MMAC). This dataset covers classification, segmentation, and spherical equivalent prediction, fostering automated analysis research. Extensive experiments on the MMAC dataset reveal the superior performance of our proposed approach, which *ranked 1st* on the challenge leaderboard. This work addresses a critical need for accurate and efficient myopic maculopathy diagnosis and intervention. The code will be publicly available at https://github.com/FDU-VTS/MMAC.

Keywords: Myopic Maculopathy · Plus Lesions Segmentation · Model Ensemble · Deep Learning

1 Introduction

Myopia is a prevalent ocular condition that impacts substantial populations worldwide [6]. Moreover, myopia can progress into high myopia, where visual

This work was supported by the National Natural Science Foundation of China (No. 62172101), Chinese National key research and development program (Project number 2021YFC2702100) and Science and Technology Commission of Shanghai Municipality (No. 21511104502).

B. Sheng et al. (Eds.): MICCAI 2023, LNCS 14563, pp. 46–55, 2024.
https://doi.org/10.1007/978-3-031-54857-4_4

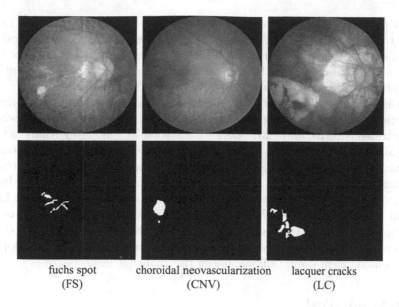

fuchs spot   choroidal neovascularization   lacquer cracks
(FS)   (CNV)   (LC)

Fig. 1. Examples of three myopic maculopathy plus lesions in the MMAC dataset.

impairment primarily stems from the emergence of diverse forms of myopic maculopathy [11,21]. In numerous nations, myopic maculopathy stands out as a prominent contributor to global visual impairment and legal blindness [17,24]. Myopic maculopathy can be classified into five categories according to the severity [17]. Furthermore, within these categories, three supplementary "Plus" lesions have been identified and incorporated, namely lacquer cracks (LC), choroidal neovascularization (CNV), and fuchs spot (FS). It is worth noting that myopic maculopathy tends to exhibit accelerated progression after reaching the tessellated fundus stage [21]. An estimated 90% of eyes affected by CNV are observed to experience a progression of myopic maculopathy [21]. Currently, the prevailing imaging modality for diagnosing myopic maculopathy is fundus photography. This modality offers the ability to facilitate accurate and swift myopic maculopathy diagnosis. Timely screening and intervention are imperative to mitigate the progressive nature of myopic maculopathy and prevent vision loss. However, the diagnostic process for myopic maculopathy remains hindered by the laborious and expertise-dependent manual inspection of individual images. Consequently, the development of an effective computer-aided system is essential to assist ophthalmologists in the comprehensive analysis of myopic maculopathy, thereby enhancing diagnostic precision and facilitating well-founded intervention strategies for this condition.

Recently, deep learning approaches have achieved promising performance in fundus image analysis [7,9,16], where lesion segmentation is one of the important tasks. However, the majority of fundus lesions segmentation focuses on diabetic retinopathy (DR) [3,15,23], age-related macular degeneration (AMD) [4,13], and glaucoma [2,20]. The lack of datasets pertaining to myopic maculopathy plus lesions has resulted in a limited repertoire of methodologies for the segmentation of such lesions. Moreover, given the substantial structural disparities among lesions, conventional fundus segmentation methods prove inadequate for myopic maculopathy plus lesions. Therefore, the development of a more robust methodology is imperative to bridge this gap in research.

In this work, we propose an ensemble of deep learning approaches for myopic maculopathy plus lesions segmentation on fundus images. Our methods are demonstrated effective in the MICCAI 2023 Myopic Maculopathy Analysis Challenge (MMAC). It is the first public dataset that covers the classification and segmentation of myopic maculopathy, and the prediction of spherical equivalent, with fundus images. Figure 1 illustrates some examples from the plus lesions segmentation of myopic maculopathy subset with different lesions masks. In our solution, we develop an ensemble of deep learning methods with strong data augmentation for training. Extensive experiments on the MMAC dataset show that our proposed solutions achieve superior performance for myopic maculopathy plus lesions segmentation, ranking 1st on the challenge leaderboard.

2   Related Work

Deep learning methods have been demonstrated considerable efficacy in the segmentation of fundus lesions. For DR lesions segmentation, Huang et al. [10] introduced a Relation Transformer Block that employs self-attention and cross-attention transformers. The self-attention transformer captured global dependencies among lesion features, while the cross-attention transformer integrated vascular information to enhance lesion detection in complex fundus structures. Guo et al. [5] proposed a multi-scale feature fusion method for small lesion regions, ensuring a high-level network response. They also employed a multi-channel bin loss to address class and loss imbalances. For AMD lesions segmentation, Kamble et al. [12] proposed a lesion-aware adversarial deep network (LADeN) that outperformed existing methods in retinal disease diagnosis by effectively incorporating lesion information for lesions segmentation. For glaucoma lesions segmentation, Pascal et al. [18] introduced an innovative multi-task deep learning model that capitalizes on the shared characteristics of related eye-fundus tasks and measurements utilized in glaucoma diagnosis. The model concurrently acquired knowledge in various segmentation and classification tasks, leveraging their inherent similarities for enhanced performance.

However, there are still few studies on myopic maculopathy plus lesions segmentation. Tang et al. [22] developed deep learning models utilizing color fundus photographs for the automatic grading of myopic maculopathy, pathologic myopia diagnosis, and precise identification and segmentation of myopia-related lesions. To the best of our knowledge, this study represents the sole endeavor in the realm of myopic maculopathy plus lesions segmentation. Therefore, the myopic maculopathy plus lesions segmentation method remains to be explored.

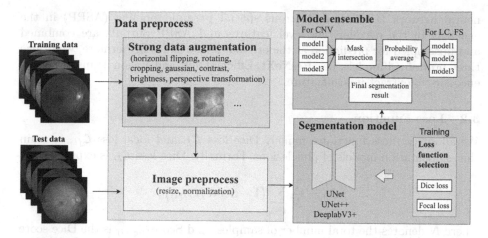

Fig. 2. Components analyzed in our deep learning framework for myopic maculopathy plus lesions segmentation. The framework consists of data preprocessing (yellow area), segmentation models with different model backbones and training approaches (red area), and model ensemble methods (purple area). (Color figure online)

3 Methodology

The proposed framework is shown in Fig. 2. We adopt the UNet [19], UNet++ [25] and DeeplabV3+ [1] networks with various pre-trained encoders for myopic maculopathy plus lesions segmentation. Except for the slightly different ensemble method for CNV lesions, the same strategy is designed to train segmentation models for three different lesions. As we do not split the validation set, very strong data augmentation is applied to prevent overfitting. In particular, we use two different data augmentations to improve the performance of the model. Besides, we employ the model ensemble strategy when predicting the segmented masks of lesions. In the following section, we will introduce the UNet, UNet++ and DeeplabV3+ networks, pre-trained encoder and loss functions.

3.1 Network Architecture

(1) UNet [19] is a neural network that combines an encoder, featuring down-sampling layers, with a decoder that incorporates up-sampling layers and includes skip connections. (2) UNet++ [25] introduces an innovative approach that involves assembling multiple U-Nets with varying depths efficiently. This ensemble model partly shares an encoder and co-learns by incorporating deep supervision. Moreover, UNet++ introduces a novel redesign of skip connections, which leverages multi-scale semantic features, resulting in a versatile feature aggregation strategy. (3) DeeplabV3+ [1] employs an encoder-decoder architecture for image segmentation. The encoder extracts features, reducing the feature map and capturing high-level semantics. The decoder reconstructs spatial information and pixel classification. The network comprises a deep convolutional

neural network (DCNN) and atrous spatial pyramid pooling (ASPP) in the encoder. In the decoder, low-level features and ASPP outputs are combined and upsampled for prediction at the original resolution. Furthermore, we utilize three pretrained models, i.e., ResNeXt, EfficientNet, and Vision Transformer, as encoders to extract image features.

3.2 Loss Function

We adopt two loss functions, namely Dice loss $\mathcal{L}_D$ and focal loss $\mathcal{L}_{fl}$, to train the segmentation models of plus lesions. Formally, Dice loss $\mathcal{L}_D$ is expressed by:

$$\mathcal{L}_D = \frac{1}{N} \sum_{i=1}^{N} \left(1 - \text{Score}_{Dice(i)}\right), \tag{1}$$

where N denotes the total number of samples, and $\text{Score}_{Dice(i)}$ is the Dice score of sample x_i. The focal loss [14] is a specialized loss function crafted to tackle the issues related to class imbalance and challenging samples in classification tasks. It incorporates a modulating factor into the standard cross-entropy loss to assign increased importance to incorrectly classified samples while gradually diminishing the weight assigned to well-classified samples, which is defined as:

$$\mathcal{L}_{fl}(y, \hat{y}) = -\frac{1}{N} \sum_{i=1}^{N} \alpha_i (1 - \hat{y}_i)^{\gamma} \log \hat{y}_i, \tag{2}$$

where α_i is a balancing factor and γ is a focusing parameter. We train the networks by each loss function or a joint loss function for the segmentation of three lesions.

3.3 Model Ensemble

The model ensemble is utilized to enhance overall performance and generalization by aggregating predictions from multiple individual models. This technique has proved to be effective in previous competitions [8]. Diverse ensemble strategies encompass voting, bagging, boosting, and stacking. In this work, for CNV, the final result is obtained by taking the intersection of the masks generated by all the models. For the other two lesions, the results of all models are directly fused to obtain the final result.

4   Experiments

4.1   Dataset

The MMAC dataset for the segmentation of myopic maculopathy plus lesions contains three different myopic maculopathy plus lesions, i.e., lacquer cracks (LC), choroidal neovascularization (CNV) and fuchs spot (FS). Table 1 shows the number of images on the segmentation subset of the MMAC dataset, including the data distribution of the training set, validation set, and test set from two data centers.

Table 1. Segmentation dataset of MMAC challenge. (Data Center 1/2)

Lesions	Training set	Validation set	Test set
Lacquer Cracks	63 (21/42)	12 (5/7)	46 (21/25)
Choroidal Neovascularization	32 (5/27)	7 (2/5)	22 (4/18)
Fuchs Spot	54 (21/33)	13 (6/7)	45 (20/25)

Table 2. Results on the validation set. The data augmentation (DA) 2 is little stronger than 1.

ID	Method	Encoder	Loss	Intersection	DA	LC DSC	CNV DSC	FS DSC	Average
1	Unet&Unet++	ResNeXt	Dice	✗	1	0.7057	0.6230	0.7741	0.7009
2†	Unet&Unet++	ResNeXt	Dice	✗	1	0.6828	0.6404	0.7835	0.7022
3†	Unet&Unet++	ResNeXt	Dice	✗	1	0.7000	0.5857	**0.7997**	0.6951
4	Unet&Unet++	ResNeXt	Dice	✓	1	0.6903	0.6289	0.7791	0.6995
5	Unet&Unet++	ResNeXt	Dice &focal	✗	1	0.6916	0.5748	0.7193	0.6619
6	Unet&Unet++ &DeeplabV3+	ResNeXt	Dice	✗	2	**0.7102**	0.5860	0.7952	0.6971
7	Unet&Unet++	EfficientNet	Dice	✗	1	0.6488	0.5249	0.7428	0.6388
8	Unet&Unet++	ViT	Dice	✗	1	0.6806	0.5724	0.7635	0.6722
9	Ensemble 1,2			✓		0.6460	**0.6988**	0.7878	0.7109

† The network was re-trained by a different random seed.

4.2 Implementation Details

All images resized to 512×512 are fed to UNet and UNet++. Strong data augmentation includes horizontal flipping, rotating, random cropping, gaussian noise, perspective, and color jittering. All images are normalized by mean = [0.485, 0.456, 0.406] and std = [0.229, 0.224, 0.225]. The networks are optimized using the Adam algorithm and trained for 100 epochs. The initial learning rate is set to 1e−4, and we use step learning rate schedule. The methods were implemented on the PyTorch platform and run on Tesla V100 GPUs.

4.3 Evaluation Metrics

Following the same protocol as the MMAC challenge, we adopt the Dice metric to evaluate our model on the training set and choose the best model.

4.4 Results on the Validation Set

The results of our models on the validation set are shown in Table 2. From the first three rows of Table 2, it's evident that there's considerable variability in the performance on the validation set, even when using the same model. In comparison to ID 3, ID 4 is an ensemble method incorporating intersection. Observably, this leads to enhanced segmentation results for CNV. Incorporating focal loss into ID 5 diminishes its impact, yet it proves effective in enhancing the overall

Table 3. Top-8 results on the MMAC challenge leaderboard.

Rank	Team Name	LC DSC	CNV DSC	FS DSC	Average
1	**fdvts_mm (ours)**	0.6651 (3)	**0.6733 (1)**	**0.8409 (1)**	**0.7264 (1)**
2	latim	0.6838 (2)	0.6557 (2)	0.8348 (2)	0.7248 (2)
3	hyeonminkim0625	**0.6865** (1)	0.6490 (4)	0.8317 (3)	0.7224 (3)
4	AIFuture	0.6440 (6)	0.6527 (3)	0.8149 (4)	0.7039 (4)
5	UR	0.6641 (4)	0.5793 (5)	0.7684 (6)	0.6706 (5)
6	dj28	0.6600 (5)	0.5452 (6)	0.7908 (5)	0.6653 (6)
7	Black	0.6220 (7)	0.4659 (7)	0.7346 (8)	0.6075 (7)
8	fdlzlab	0.6189 (8)	0.3313 (8)	0.7429 (7)	0.5644 (8)

generalization capability of the model within the final ensemble. Similar to ID 5, ID 6 aims to enhance generalization by introducing additional models and implementing more robust data augmentation techniques. ID 7 and ID 8 clearly demonstrate that ResNeXt emerges as the most effective encoder, delivering superior results. In conclusion, for LC, Model ID 6 yields the most favorable outcomes. For CNV, Model ID 9 exhibits the top results. For FS, Model ID 3 demonstrates superior performance. Therefore, in the testing phase, we selected ID 3, 5, 9 as the segmentation models of CNV, and ID 3, 5, 6 as the segmentation models of LC and FS.

4.5   Results on the Leaderboard

Table 3 shows the top-8 results of our method and other participants on the testing set of task 2 in the MMAC challenge. Our ensembled method ranked 1st on the leaderboard, approaching 0.7264 mDice.

4.6   Visual Segmentation Results

Figure 3 visually compares the best results on the validation set and the best results on the test set for the three plus lesions. For the validation, the models corresponding to the results in bold in Table 1 are visualized, and for the test, the best models that we submitted during the testing phase are visualized. As shown in Fig. 3, for FS and LC, the red circles denote instances where models submitted during the testing phase yield superior results, implying that greater integration of models leads to improved outcomes. For CNV, the ensemble method of intersection produces higher final metrics due to the substantial area of the predicted mask compared to the smaller area of the ground-truth mask.

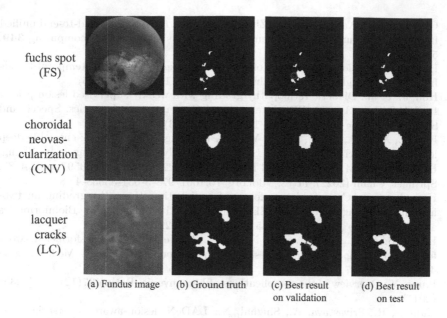

| | (a) Fundus image | (b) Ground truth | (c) Best result on validation | (d) Best result on test |

Fig. 3. Visual segmentation result of different lesions and models.

5 Conclusion

In conclusion, myopic maculopathy is a prevalent and visually debilitating condition, necessitating timely diagnosis and intervention. However, manual image analysis is labor-intensive and experience-dependent. This study presents an ensemble of deep learning solutions for myopic maculopathy plus lesions segmentation, achieving top-ranking performance in the MICCAI 2023 MMAC challenge. Our results underscore the potential of deep learning in revolutionizing the diagnosis and management of myopic maculopathy, offering a ray of hope for patients and ophthalmologists alike.

References

1. Chen, L.-C., Zhu, Y., Papandreou, G., Schroff, F., Adam, H.: Encoder-decoder with atrous separable convolution for semantic image segmentation. In: Ferrari, V., Hebert, M., Sminchisescu, C., Weiss, Y. (eds.) ECCV 2018. LNCS, vol. 11211, pp. 833–851. Springer, Cham (2018). https://doi.org/10.1007/978-3-030-01234-2_49
2. Coan, L.J., et al.: Automatic detection of glaucoma via fundus imaging and artificial intelligence: a review. Surv. Ophthalmol. **68**(1), 17–41 (2023)
3. Dai, L., et al.: A deep learning system for detecting diabetic retinopathy across the disease spectrum. Nat. Commun. **12**(1), 3242 (2021)
4. Fang, H., et al.: Adam challenge: Detecting age-related macular degeneration from fundus images. IEEE Trans. Med. Imaging **41**(10), 2828–2847 (2022). https://doi.org/10.1109/TMI.2022.3172773

5. Guo, S., Li, T., Kang, H., Li, N., Zhang, Y., Wang, K.: L-Seg: an end-to-end unified framework for multi-lesion segmentation of fundus images. Neurocomputing **349**, 52–63 (2019)
6. Holden, B.A.: Global prevalence of myopia and high myopia and temporal trends from 2000 through 2050. Ophthalmology **123**(5), 1036–1042 (2016)
7. Hou, J., et al.: Diabetic retinopathy grading with weakly-supervised lesion priors. In: ICASSP 2023–2023 IEEE International Conference on Acoustics, Speech and Signal Processing (ICASSP), pp. 1–5. IEEE (2023)
8. Hou, J., Xiao, F., Xu, J., Zhang, Y., Zou, H., Feng, R.: Deep-octa: ensemble deep learning approaches for diabetic retinopathy analysis on octa images. In: Sheng, B., Aubreville, M. (eds.) MIDOG DRAC 2022 2022. LNCS, vol. 13597, pp. 74–87. Springer, Cham (2022). https://doi.org/10.1007/978-3-031-33658-4_8
9. Hou, J., et al.: Cross-field transformer for diabetic retinopathy grading on two-field fundus images. In: 2022 IEEE International Conference on Bioinformatics and Biomedicine (BIBM), pp. 985–990. IEEE (2022)
10. Huang, S., Li, J., Xiao, Y., Shen, N., Xu, T.: RTNet: relation transformer network for diabetic retinopathy multi-lesion segmentation. IEEE Trans. Med. Imaging **41**(6), 1596–1607 (2022)
11. Ikuno, Y.: Overview of the complications of high myopia. Retina **37**(12), 2347–2351 (2017)
12. Kamble, R., Srivastava, A., Singhal, N.: LADeN: lesion-aware adversarial deep network for grading of macular diseases using color fundus images. In: 2022 IEEE 19th International Symposium on Biomedical Imaging (ISBI), pp. 1–4. IEEE (2022)
13. Li, P., Liang, L., Gao, Z., Wang, X.: AMD-Net: automatic subretinal fluid and hemorrhage segmentation for wet age-related macular degeneration in ocular fundus images. Biomed. Signal Process. Control **80**, 104262 (2023). https://doi.org/10.1016/j.bspc.2022.104262. https://www.sciencedirect.com/science/article/pii/S1746809422007169
14. Lin, T.Y., Goyal, P., Girshick, R., He, K., Dollár, P.: Focal loss for dense object detection. In: Proceedings of the IEEE International Conference on Computer Vision, pp. 2980–2988 (2017)
15. Liu, Q., Liu, H., Ke, W., Liang, Y.: Automated lesion segmentation in fundus images with many-to-many reassembly of features. Pattern Recogn. **136**, 109191 (2023)
16. Liu, R., et al.: DeepDRiD: diabetic retinopathy-grading and image quality estimation challenge. Patterns **3**(6), 100512 (2022)
17. Ohno-Matsui, K., et al.: International photographic classification and grading system for myopic maculopathy. Am. J. Ophthalmol. **159**(5), 877–883 (2015)
18. Pascal, L., Perdomo, O.J., Bost, X., Huet, B., Otálora, S., Zuluaga, M.A.: Multi-task deep learning for glaucoma detection from color fundus images. Sci. Rep. **12**(1), 12361 (2022)
19. Ronneberger, O., Fischer, P., Brox, T.: U-Net: convolutional networks for biomedical image segmentation. In: Navab, N., Hornegger, J., Wells, W.M., Frangi, A.F. (eds.) MICCAI 2015. LNCS, vol. 9351, pp. 234–241. Springer, Cham (2015). https://doi.org/10.1007/978-3-319-24574-4_28
20. Shyamalee, T., Meedeniya, D.: Glaucoma detection with retinal fundus images using segmentation and classification. Mach. Intell. Res. **19**(6), 563–580 (2022)
21. Silva, R.: Myopic maculopathy: a review. Ophthalmologica **228**(4), 197–213 (2012)
22. Tang, J., et al.: An artificial-intelligence-based automated grading and lesions segmentation system for myopic maculopathy based on color fundus photographs. Trans. Vis. Sci. Technol. **11**(6), 16 (2022)

23. Xue, W., et al.: Deep learning-based analysis of infrared fundus photography for automated diagnosis of diabetic retinopathy with cataracts. J. Cataract Refract. Surg. **49**(10), 1043–1048 (2023)
24. Yokoi, T., Ohno-Matsui, K.: Diagnosis and treatment of myopic maculopathy. Asia-Pac. J. Ophthalmol. **7**(6), 415–421 (2018)
25. Zhou, Z., Rahman Siddiquee, M.M., Tajbakhsh, N., Liang, J.: UNet++: a nested U-net architecture for medical image segmentation. In: Stoyanov, D., et al. (eds.) DLMIA/ML-CDS -2018. LNCS, vol. 11045, pp. 3–11. Springer, Cham (2018). https://doi.org/10.1007/978-3-030-00889-5_1

Beyond MobileNet: An Improved MobileNet for Retinal Diseases

Wenhui Zhu[1](✉)(ID), Peijie Qiu[2], Xiwen Chen[3], Huayu Li[4], Hao Wang[3], Natasha Lepore[6], Oana M. Dumitrascu[5], and Yalin Wang[1](ID)

[1] School of Computing and Augmented Intelligence, Arizona State University, Tempe, AZ, USA
wzhu59@asu.edu
[2] McKeley School of Engineering, Washington University in St. Louis, St. Louis, MO, USA
[3] School of Computing, Clemson University, Clemson, SC, USA
[4] Department of Electrical and Computer Engineering, The University of Arizona, Tucson, AZ, USA
[5] Department of Neurology, Mayo Clinic, Phoenix, AZ, USA
[6] CIBORG Lab, Department of Radiology, Children's Hospital Los Angeles, Los Angeles, CA, USA

Abstract. Myopic Maculopathy (MM) is the leading cause of severe vision loss or blindness. Deep learning-based automated tools are indispensable in assisting clinicians in diagnosing and monitoring RD in modern medicine. Recently, an increasing number of works in this field have taken advantage of Vision Transformer to achieve state-of-the-art performance with more parameters and higher model complexity compared to Convolutional Neural Networks (CNNs). Such sophisticated model designs, however, are prone to be overfitting and hinder their advantages in specific tasks in medical image analysis. In this work, we argue that a well-calibrated CNN model may mitigate these problems. To this end, we empirically investigated the macro and micro designs of a CNN and its training strategies by starting with a standard MobileNet. Based on the investigation, we proposed a lightweight MobileNet training framework equipped with a series of optimal parameters and modules based on retinal images. As a result of performance, our model secured third place in the MICCAI MMAC 2023 Challenge - Classification of Myopic Maculopathy. Our software package is available at https://github.com/Retinal-Research/NN-MOBILENET

Keywords: Retinal Diseases · Fundus image · Classification · MICCAI MMAC (Myopic Maculopathy Analysis Challenge) 2023

1 Introduction

Retinal diseases (RD), particularly myopic maculopathy, are leading causes of blindness globally [8,27]. The automated RD diagnosis framework is crucial in

B. Sheng et al. (Eds.): MICCAI 2023, LNCS 14563, pp. 56–65, 2024.
https://doi.org/10.1007/978-3-031-54857-4_5

modern medicine to guide the proper treatment of patients. In the past decade, due to the strong ability, deep learning, such as convolutional neural networks (CNNs) and Vision Transformers (ViT) [11], have achieved state-of-the-art performance in various computer vision tasks. Due to this nature, DL-based methods have been widely used in the applications of retinal disease diagnosis, such as retinal image quality enhancement [34, 35], lesion segmentation [1, 23] and automated diagnosis [4, 14, 36]. These advancements have not only refined the accuracy of diagnoses but have also streamlined the process, leading to faster and more reliable patient care.

In the context of applications, the classification of myopic maculopathy is one of the most essential tasks since it can offer the initial assessment of severity and allow more effective tailored interventions. To advance the classification performance, in this work, a series of experimental investigations were conducted on the MobileNet architecture to ascertain the optimal modules and parameter configurations. The impetus behind our investigation derives from a two-fold perspective. Firstly, addressing the issue of model overfitting, like data augmentation. Secondly, it strives to comprehensively leverage channel-wise information by means of selecting channel-aware modules, such as spatial dropout [22], channel attention [25], and channel configuration [6]. Based on our investigation, we proposed a fine-tuned lightweight MobileNet based on retinal images and studied its performance in various retinal image datasets. The contribution of this paper can be summarized into two aspects. Firstly, we addressed a common overfitting issue in fundus image classification tasks by introducing dropout modules based on channel-wise information and combining heavy data augmentation. In particular, our study presented a counterintuitive result that heavy data augmentation helped improve performance, unlike the prevailing belief that heavy data augmentation disrupted the structure of medical images. Secondly, based on our investigation, we proposed a series of modifications to MobileNetv2 [20] that demonstrated remarkable improvements in the classification of retinal diseases. Our method did not rely on complex multitasking but instead inherited its simple and efficient characteristics. It is worth noting that we did not use this dataset in this challenge for pretrainING. Basically, the model was designed from the proposed method in myopic maculopathy application [36].

2 Related Work

2.1 CNN-Based Method for RD Diagnosis

Convolutional neural networks (CNNs) are the most popular architecture in RD-related diagnosis [2, 12, 13, 19, 24, 32, 33] and were dominating the early stages of development. Many studies have incorporated prior knowledge of the retinal lesion or the clinician-provided diagnosis into CNNs. Zoom-in-Net [24] took a biomimetic approach that used image magnification to locate lesions in the diagnosis of RD. Zhou et al. proposed a semi-supervised learning framework [32], which coordinated lesion segmentation and classification tasks by feature integrations. CANet [12] integrated two attention modules to jointly generate disease-specific and disease-dependent features for grading DR and diabetic macular edema (DME). Che et al. [2] achieved good performance via robust disentangled features of DR/DME. While these methods have demonstrated promising results, their complex and task-specific model designs were easy to overfitting and required specific datasets (e.g., multi-task datasets). Recently, Wen et al. [36] introduced a series of fine-tuned based on MobileNetV2, a non-new MobileNet achieving state-of-the-art (SOTA) results on multiple retinal disease datasets.

2.2   VIT-Based Method for RD Diagnosis

Vision Transformers (ViT) have recently gained much attention in various visual tasks by leveraging the self-attention mechanism to capture long-term feature dependencies. Along this direction, MIL-VT [28] proposed using multiple-instance pooling to aggregate the features extracted by a ViT. Sun et al. [21] proposed a lesion-aware transformer (LAT) to learn the diabetic lesion-specific features via a cross-attention mechanism. To reduce the model complexity of transformer-based methods, Jiang et al. [10] proposed an efficient transformer design (SatFormer) by taking advantage of an efficient abnormality-aware attention mechanism and a saliency enhancement module for DR grading. Although those methods achieved state-of-the-art performance, most of them heavily relied on pretraining on large-scale datasets due to the data-hungry nature of ViT, whose complexity quadratically grew with respect to the input size. In addition, the RD features are localized in nature. It was challenging for pure transformer-based feature extractors to focus more on global representations. To mitigate this issue, recent ViT advances [15,18] converged to CNNs on bringing back convolutional operations. This motivated us to rethink the role of CNN in designing RD diagnostic models.

3   Methods

Guided by the hypothesis that channel-wise information played a crucial role in improving diagnostic performance for RD, our CNN architecture upon MobileNetv2 [20] used deepwise convolution and channel attention in each residual building block. We also empirically investigated optimizing the number of channels and incorporating Dropout in each residual building block to enhance the generalizability and prevent overfitting. To further address the overfitting problem, we adopted a heavy data-augmentation approach. Additionally, we explored the activation and optimizer to improve the performance further. Here, we used the **Messidor-2 dataset** [5] for the empirical studies, which contained 1748 fundus images with five DR grades.

3.1   Network Design

Inverted Linear Residual Block (ILRB): The original residual building block followed a trend of sequentially widening, narrowing, and finally widening the number of channels. Many modern designs of CNNs [6,16,20], however,

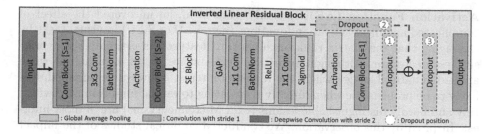

Fig. 1. Inverted linear residual block (ILRB) architecture design.

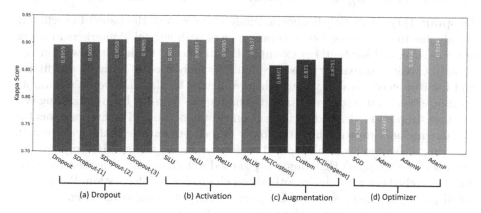

Fig. 2. Single parameter empirical studies based on Messidor 2. We keep the other parameters consistent in each experiment, but it does not mean the other parameters are the best. MC denote Mixup [30] and CutMix [29], and SpatialDropout-[x] denote Placement in position x

inverted this order with a narrow to wide to narrow channel configuration by taking advantage of deep-wise convolution, namely inverted residual block (IRB). By further discarding the activation function after the last convolutional layer to prevent information loss during the rectified linear unit (ReLU) activation, the IRB turned to an inverted linear residual block (ILRB). The deepwise convolution performed separate 2D convolution on a per-channel basis and then weighted the feature map of each channel by a 1×1 convolution to aggregate the channel dimension, which resembled the Convolutional Block Attention Module in [26]. To further capture the channel-wise information, the Squeeze-and-Excitation block in [9] was adopted to each residual block. We kept the same stem setting (i.e., channel configuration and the number of filters) of each ILRB as that in [6] with an expansion rate of 1 for the first ILRB and 6 otherwise. The expansion rate denotes the rate of channel dimensions between the hidden layers and the input to each ILRB module. Figure 1 shows the detailed structure of the ILRB module. The effectiveness of this module was also demonstrated in subsequent ablation experiments.

Activation Function (AF): Recently, Han et al. [6] uncovered the effect of complicated nonlinear activation functions (e.g., ELU or SiLU) in visual tasks by leveraging that the matrix rank of the output feature can estimate the expressiveness of a layer. Although surprising performance has been achieved when applied in natural images where the region of interest is always well-defined, it is likely to be problematic when directly translating to retinal fundus images where tiny and hardly distinguishable lesions (e.g., Microaneurysms) are of most interest. Inspired by this observation, We conducted empirical studies of the impact of different activation functions (i.e., SiLU, ReLU, PReLU, ReLU6) on RD tasks. As shown in Fig. 2(B), the ReLU6 activation was the best among all options.

Dropout (D): Most RD diagnostic models suffer from the issue of overfitting mainly due to the heterogeneous appearance of pathological biomarkers in terms of size, shape, and location. For example, DR diagnostic models are always struggling to classify Microaneurysms. Dropout is widely used to mitigate overfitting and improve generalizability. But where and how to place Dropouts remain an open question. In this study, we tried to answer this question by investigating two common dropout modes and their positions in the network. The first one was the regular random dropout which randomly zeroed out entries in the feature map following a Bernoulli distribution. The second mode was spatial-dropout [22] (channel-wise dropout) that randomly zeroed out channels in the feature map, which matched our previous hypothesis on channel-wise information. We investigated three possible locations of Dropout placement in the ILRB (Fig. 1) where location 3 showed the best performance (Fig. 2(A)).

3.2   Training Techniques

Data Augmentations (DA): Most previous work [10,12,21,28] held the view that excessive data augmentation could potentially compromise the integrity of fundus data. Therefore, data augmentations including spatial transformations and brightness adjustments were always recommended in retinal fundus images. Nevertheless, these data augmentations could not eliminate overfitting in the RD tasks based on our empirical studies. Building upon the aforementioned observations, exploratory experiments were conducted to optimize the data augmentation strategies that better prevent overfitting. We presented three data augmentation combinations: (I). Customized data augmentations in methods [10,21]; (II). Customized data augmentations in methods [10,21] with Mixup [30] and CutMix [29]; (III). The official ImageNet data augmentation techniques [16] (e.g., RandAugment [3] and Random Erasing [31]) with Mixup and CutMix. Our empirical studies showed that the heaviest data augmentations (III) led to the best performance (Fig. 2(C)).

Optimizer (O): Recent empirical studies demonstrated that performance improvement was gained by training the neural networks with more advanced optimizers (e.g., AdamW [17], AdamP [7]) that better accommodated the step size adaptively. As shown in Fig. 2(D), our empirical studies showed that training the network with AdamP optimizers significantly increased the performance.

Fig. 3. Beyond Mobile model framework.

Table 1. All training configuration for Beyond MobileNet

Training configuration	Beyond MobileNet
ILRB stem setting (Channel configuration in Fig. 3)	$(3, 96, 48, 82, 116, 149, 183,$ $217, 250, 284, 318, 352, 386$ $, 419, 453, 487, 520, 554)$
Activation Function replacement in ILRB	ReLu6
Dropout Adding	Spatial-Dropout at position 3
Data Augmentation	ResizedCrop, HorizontalFlip
	AutoContras, Equalize, Invert
	Rotate, Posterize, Solarize
	Color, Sharpness, Shear
	Brightness, RandomErasing,
	Translate + mixup and cutmix
Optimizer	AdamP
batch size	64
learning rate	0.001
weight decay	0.005
scheduler	cosine decay 20 epoch warmup from $1e-6$
Dropout rate	0.15
mixup	0.8
cutmix	1.0
epoch	1000
loss	cross-entropy

4 MMAC - Classification of Myopic Maculopathy

4.1 Dataset and Evaluation Metrics

The challenge contains 1143 fundus images with four myopic maculopathy grades. There are 404 images for grade 0, 412 images for grade 1, 224 images for grade 2, 60 images for grade 3, and 43 images for grade 4. We used 5-fold stratified cross-validation on the training set. The Quadratic-weighted Kappa (kappa), F1 score, and Specificity were used as the evaluation metric. For this experiment, we felt the raw data was good quality and did not need to apply any preprocessing, and the 224×224 image size served as the input for the network. The best model weight would be selected based on the average of kappa, F1, and specificity.

Table 2. Best model weights performed at official validation set.

Method	kappa	F1 score	Specificity	average	CPU time
Weight1	0.8474	0.7598	0.9252	0.8442	0.1084
Weight2	0.8191	0.7492	0.9268	0.8317	0.1128
Weight3	0.8183	0.7555	0.9307	0.8349	0.1108
Ensemble with max	0.8162	0.7569	0.9275	0.8335	0.2843
Ensemble with average	0.8675	0.8091	0.9354	0.8707	0.3017

Table 3. Final challenge rank based on official testing set.

Team	kappa	F1 score	Specificity	average	CPU time
Rank 1st	0.9005	0.7807	0.9445	0.8752	2.1283
Rank 2nd	0.8893	0.7681	0.9406	0.8660	0.8047
Ours (Rank 3rd)	0.8995	0.7513	0.9407	0.8638	0.2750

4.2   Implementation Details

An optimal set of network structures and training strategies is summarized in Sect. 3. We used cross-entropy loss for training all the models in this work. The initial learning rate was set to 0.001 decayed according to a cosine decay learning rate scheduler with 20 epochs of linear warm-up. A weight decay rate of 0.005 was applied to prevent further overfitting. All experiments were performed on three GeForce RTX 3090 with a batch size of 64 and 1000 epochs. All were implemented in PyTorch. Here is the conclusion for all training configurations for Beyond MobileNet as shown in Table 1

4.3   Experimental Results

In this challenge, we submit each best model weight to the platform for evaluation. As shown in Table 2, three are the top three performance model weights of Beyond MobileNet. We perform the ensemble operation based on three weights. The max denoted selected the maximal output value for each class between three weights, and the average applied the average based on the three-weight output as the final prediction. The ensemble with average outperforms the other weights, which served as the final submission version. As shown in Table 3, The model achieved third place in this challenge.

5   Conclusion

In this paper, we provided novel insights into the RD diagnostic model design informed by the channel-wise information in retinal fundus images. A generic and efficient CNN-based architecture design and its training strategies were proposed for general RD tasks. Our comprehensive experimental results demonstrated that a properly tuned CNN rather than a model with a large number of parameters and complex structures could achieve a competitive result.

References

1. Arega, T.W., Legrand, F., Bricq, S., Meriaudeau, F.: Using MRI-specific data augmentation to enhance the segmentation of right ventricle in multi-disease, multi-center and multi-view cardiac MRI. In: Puyol Antón, E., et al. (eds.) STACOM 2021. LNCS, vol. 13131, pp. 250–258. Springer, Cham (2022). https://doi.org/10.1007/978-3-030-93722-5_27
2. Che, H., Jin, H., Chen, H.: Learning robust representation for joint grading of ophthalmic diseases via adaptive curriculum and feature disentanglement. In: Wang, L., Dou, Q., Fletcher, P.T., Speidel, S., Li, S. (eds.) MICCAI 2022. LNCS, vol. 13433, pp. 523–533. Springer, Cham (2022). https://doi.org/10.1007/978-3-031-16437-8_50
3. Cubuk, E.D., Zoph, B., et al.: RandAugment: practical automated data augmentation with a reduced search space. In: Proceedings of the IEEE/CVF Conference on Computer Vision and Pattern Recognition Workshops, pp. 702–703 (2020)
4. Dai, L., et al.: A deep learning system for detecting diabetic retinopathy across the disease spectrum. Nat. Commun. 12(1), 3242 (2021)
5. Decencière, E., et al.: Feedback on a publicly distributed image database: the Messidor database. Image Anal. Stereol. 33, 231–234 (2014)
6. Han, D., Yun, S., Heo, B., Yoo, Y.: Rethinking channel dimensions for efficient model design. In: Proceedings of the IEEE/CVF Conference on Computer Vision and Pattern Recognition, pp. 732–741 (2021)
7. Heo, B., et al.: AdamP: slowing down the slowdown for momentum optimizers on scale-invariant weights. arXiv preprint arXiv:2006.08217 (2020)
8. Holden, B.A., et al.: Global prevalence of myopia and high myopia and temporal trends from 2000 through 2050. Ophthalmology 123(5), 1036–1042 (2016)
9. Hu, J., Shen, L., Sun, G.: Squeeze-and-excitation networks. In: Proceedings of the IEEE Conference on Computer Vision and Pattern Recognition, pp. 7132–7141 (2018)
10. Jiang, Y., et al.: Satformer: saliency-guided abnormality-aware transformer for retinal disease classification in fundus image. In: Proceedings of the Thirty-First International Joint Conference on Artificial Intelligence, IJCAI, pp. 987–994 (2022)
11. Khan, S., Naseer, M., Hayat, M., Zamir, S.W., Khan, F.S., Shah, M.: Transformers in vision: a survey. ACM Comput. Surv. (CSUR) 54(10s), 1–41 (2022)
12. Li, X., Hu, X., Yu, L., Zhu, L., Fu, C.W., Heng, P.A.: CANet: cross-disease attention network for joint diabetic retinopathy and diabetic macular edema grading. IEEE Trans. Med. Imaging 39, 1483–1493 (2020)
13. Lin, Z., et al.: A framework for identifying diabetic retinopathy based on anti-noise detection and attention-based fusion. In: Frangi, A.F., Schnabel, J.A., Davatzikos, C., Alberola-López, C., Fichtinger, G. (eds.) MICCAI 2018. LNCS, vol. 11071, pp. 74–82. Springer, Cham (2018). https://doi.org/10.1007/978-3-030-00934-2_9
14. Liu, R., et al.: DeepDRiD: diabetic retinopathy-grading and image quality estimation challenge. Patterns 3(6), 100512 (2022)
15. Liu, Z., et al.: Swin transformer: hierarchical vision transformer using shifted windows. In: Proceedings of the IEEE International Conference on Computer Vision (ICCV), pp. 10012–10022 (2021)

16. Liu, Z., Mao, H., Wu, C.Y., Feichtenhofer, C., Darrell, T., Xie, S.: A ConvNet for the 2020s. In: Proceedings of the IEEE Computer Society Conference on Computer Vision and Pattern Recognition, pp. 11976–11986 (2022)
17. Loshchilov, I., Hutter, F.: Decoupled weight decay regularization. In: International Conference on Learning Representations
18. Ramachandran, P., Parmar, N., Vaswani, A., Bello, I., Levskaya, A., Shlens, J.: Stand-alone self-attention in vision models. In: Advances in Neural Information Processing Systems, vol. 32 (2019)
19. Sánchez, C.I., et al.: Evaluation of a computer-aided diagnosis system for diabetic retinopathy screening on public data. Invest. Ophthalmol. Vis. Sci. **52**(7), 4866–4871 (2011)
20. Sandler, M., Howard, A., Zhu, M., Zhmoginov, A., Chen, L.C.: MobileNetV 2: inverted residuals and linear bottlenecks. In: Proceedings of the IEEE Computer Society Conference on Computer Vision and Pattern Recognition, pp. 4510–4520 (2018)
21. Sun, R., Li, Y., Zhang, T., Mao, Z., Wu, F., Zhang, Y.: Lesion-aware transformers for diabetic retinopathy grading. In: Proceedings of the IEEE Computer Society Conference on Computer Vision and Pattern Recognition, pp. 10938–10947 (2021)
22. Tompson, J., Goroshin, R., Jain, A., LeCun, Y., Bregler, C.: Efficient object localization using convolutional networks. In: Proceedings of the IEEE Conference on Computer Vision and Pattern Recognition, pp. 648–656 (2015)
23. Uysal, E.S., Bilici, M.Ş., Zaza, B.S., Özgenç, M.Y., Boyar, O.: Exploring the limits of data augmentation for retinal vessel segmentation. arXiv preprint arXiv:2105.09365 (2021)
24. Wang, Z., Yin, Y., Shi, J., Fang, W., Li, H., Wang, X.: Zoom-in-Net: deep mining lesions for diabetic retinopathy detection. In: Descoteaux, M., Maier-Hein, L., Franz, A., Jannin, P., Collins, D.L., Duchesne, S. (eds.) MICCAI 2017. LNCS, vol. 10435, pp. 267–275. Springer, Cham (2017). https://doi.org/10.1007/978-3-319-66179-7_31
25. Woo, S., Park, J., Lee, J.-Y., Kweon, I.S.: CBAM: convolutional block attention module. In: Ferrari, V., Hebert, M., Sminchisescu, C., Weiss, Y. (eds.) ECCV 2018. LNCS, vol. 11211, pp. 3–19. Springer, Cham (2018). https://doi.org/10.1007/978-3-030-01234-2_1
26. Woo, S., Park, J., Lee, J.-Y., Kweon, I.S.: CBAM: convolutional block attention module. In: Ferrari, V., Hebert, M., Sminchisescu, C., Weiss, Y. (eds.) ECCV 2018. LNCS, vol. 11211, pp. 3–19. Springer, Cham (2018). https://doi.org/10.1007/978-3-030-01234-2_1
27. Yorston, D.: Retinal diseases and vision 2020. Commun. Eye Health **16**(46), 19–20 (2003)
28. Yu, S., et al.: MIL-VT: multiple instance learning enhanced vision transformer for fundus image classification. In: de Bruijne, M., et al. (eds.) MICCAI 2021. LNCS, vol. 12908, pp. 45–54. Springer, Cham (2021). https://doi.org/10.1007/978-3-030-87237-3_5
29. Yun, S., Han, D., Oh, S.J., Chun, S., Choe, J., Yoo, Y.: CutMix: regularization strategy to train strong classifiers with localizable features. In: Proceedings of the IEEE International Conference on Computer Vision (ICCV), pp. 6023–6032 (2019)
30. Zhang, H., Cisse, M., Dauphin, Y.N., Lopez-Paz, D.: mixup: beyond empirical risk minimization. In: International Conference on Learning Representations (2018)
31. Zhong, Z., et al.: Random erasing data augmentation. In: Proceedings of the AAAI Conference on Artificial Intelligence, vol. 34, pp. 13001–13008 (2020)

32. Zhou, Y., et al.: Collaborative learning of semi-supervised segmentation and classification for medical images. In: Proceedings of the IEEE Computer Society Conference on Computer Vision and Pattern Recognition (2019)
33. Zhu, W., et al.: Self-supervised equivariant regularization reconciles multiple instance learning: joint referable diabetic retinopathy classification and lesion segmentation. In: 18th International Symposium on Medical Information Processing and Analysis (SIPAIM) (2022)
34. Zhu, W., et al.: OTRE: where optimal transport guided unpaired image-to-image translation meets regularization by enhancing. In: Frangi, A., de Bruijne, M., Wassermann, D., Navab, N. (eds.) IPMI 2023. LNCS, vol. 13939, pp. 415–427. Springer, Cham (2023). https://doi.org/10.1007/978-3-031-34048-2_32
35. Zhu, W., Qiu, P., Farazi, M., Nandakumar, K., Dumitrascu, O.M., Wang, Y.: Optimal transport guided unsupervised learning for enhancing low-quality retinal images. arXiv preprint arXiv:2302.02991 (2023)
36. Zhu, W., Qiu, P., Lepore, N., Dumitrascu, O.M., Wang, Y.: NNMobile-Net: rethinking cnn design for deep learning-based retinopathy research. arXiv preprint arXiv:2306.01289 (2023)

Prediction of Spherical Equivalent
with Vanilla ResNet

Huayu Li[1]($\boxtimes$) (iD), Wenhui Zhu[2], Xiwen Chen[3], and Yalin Wang[2]

[1] Department of Electrical and Computer Engineering, University of Arizona,
Tucson, AZ 85721, USA
hl459@arizona.edu
[2] School of Computing and Augmented Intelligence, Arizona State University,
Tempe, AZ 85281, USA
[3] School of Computing, Clemson University, Clemson, SC, USA

Abstract. Recently, an increasing of deep learning models has been introduced to address various fundus image tasks, e.g. segmentation, classification, and enhancement. Concurrently, this emergence has been accompanied by the development of increasingly intricate model architectures and a parameter surge. However, these methods have overlooked the crucial significance of the intrinsic characteristics of the data. In this regard, we posit that a vanilla ResNet, when coupled with appropriate data augmentation, can also achieve a favorable performance. This study assesses the performance of the foundational deep learning architecture, the standard Residual Network (ResNet), in predicting Spherical Equivalent (SE) values. Spherical Equivalent (SE) is a crucial parameter in optometry employed for prescribing eyeglasses to correct vision. Our study intends to demonstrate the effectiveness of ResNet with proper data augmentations in achieving precise SE predictions without additional enhancements. Utilizing a vanilla ResNet50 model, we secured the *third* position in the Myopic Maculopathy Analysis Challenge 2023, task 3. Remarkably, our findings reveal that the unaltered deployment of ResNet yields exceptional predictive performance for estimating SE, highlighting the architectural prowess of simple models in a vital yet frequently demanding optometric context. Our software package is available at https://github.com/HuayuLiArizona/Prediction-of-Spherical-Equivalent-With-Vanilla-ResNet.

Keywords: Retinal Diseases · Fundus image · Spherical Equivalent · MICCAI MMAC (Myopic Maculopathy Analysis Challenge) 2023

1 Introduction

Myopia, also known as short-sightedness or Near-sightedness, is a common eye problem [8], where the light focuses in front of, instead of on, the retina, which results in the distant objects appearing blurry. More seriously, this disease may further progress into severe *high myopia*, which is because of the development

B. Sheng et al. (Eds.): MICCAI 2023, LNCS 14563, pp. 66–74, 2024.
https://doi.org/10.1007/978-3-031-54857-4_6

of different types of myopic maculopathy [9,14]. This eye disease has impacted significant populations worldwide and, especially in many countries, such as Japan, China, Denmark, and the United States, myopic maculopathy is one of the leading causes of visual impairment and legal blindness [13,19]. Specifically, the prediction of Spherical Equivalent (SE) [5] is a central task in the field of optometry, aiding in the determination of corrective eyeglass prescriptions for individuals with vision impairments. Accurate estimation of SE is essential to ensure optimal vision correction and enhance the quality of life for patients. This step is achieved by a manual inspection and is used to diagnose myopic maculopathy after imaging modality by fundus photography. The entire process is time-consuming and relies heavily on the experience of ophthalmologists. Therefore, it's necessary to develop an automated method for this problem.

In optometry, the application of deep learning techniques in retinal disease diagnosis [3,10,11,16,18,20,23,26] as well as SE values prediction [2,15] has gained attention in recent years. Current studies in medical image analysis tend to use complex architectures [10,16,18,20,23] and sophisticated training techniques [22] to achieve state-of-the-art results. In this paper, we take a different approach by revisiting a foundational architecture in the deep learning landscape - the Residual Network (ResNet) [6]. ResNet introduced the concept of residual blocks, which alleviate the vanishing gradient problem and enable the training of deep networks with hundreds of layers. Despite the prevalence of more intricate architectures, ResNet's architectural simplicity and effectiveness warrant its reevaluation in specialized tasks such as SE prediction.

Our primary objective is to demonstrate that a vanilla ResNet, devoid of any additional tricks or modifications, can deliver compelling performance on SE prediction tasks. By leveraging the inherent capacity of ResNet to capture intricate patterns and relationships in data, we aim to establish a benchmark for SE estimation without the need for convoluted design choices or excessive model complexity. We hypothesize that ResNet's ability to model complex relationships can be directly harnessed for accurate SE predictions, underscoring that simpler architectures can often yield impressive results.

To validate our hypothesis, we conducted comprehensive experiments on a diverse dataset of optometric measurements. We compare the performance of the vanilla ResNet with contemporary deep-learning approaches and assess its effectiveness in estimating SE values accurately. Our results reveal that the straightforward implementation of ResNet attains notable predictive capabilities, showcasing the potential for achieving remarkable results in optometric applications with minimal architectural intervention. In the subsequent sections, we present our methodology, experimental setup, and detailed results, thereby emphasizing the significance of ResNet in SE prediction and advocating for a reexamination of architectural choices in specialized domains.

2 Related Works

Deep learning was widely applied for many retinal image-related tasks, including classification [10,16] and segmentation [1,17], denoising [24,25]. Especially in retinal disease diagnosis, many studies have incorporated prior knowledge of the retinal lesion or the clinician-provided diagnosis into convolutional neural networks, which introduced more modules [10,18,23] or set multi-task learning [22]. Many other methods [16,20] also utilized vision transformer(ViT) [4] to capture long-term feature dependencies. More and more complex networks were introduced to improve the performances of various benchmarks, which main performance gain from the larger learning parameters and deeper network architecture. Recently, [12] proved that a well-calibrated CNN can outperform ViT models in natural images, which proposed a series of fine-tuning based on each component. Furthermore, [26] introduced a series of fine-tuned based on MobileNetV2, a non-new MobileNet also achieving state-of-the-art (SOTA) results on multiple retinal disease datasets. This has rekindled a reconsideration of the importance of data nature and model fine-tuning. In this paper, we also started from a vanilla Resnet without tricks or modifications and researched the intrinsic characteristics of the data, emphasizing the importance of data augmentation.

3   Methods

Data Augmentations (DA): To enhance the robustness and generalization capabilities of our model, we employed a comprehensive array of data augmentation (DA) techniques during the training process. These techniques were systematically applied to the input data, introducing variability and thereby improving the model's ability to accommodate diverse inputs. The specific DA techniques incorporated into our training regimen were as follows: **(1) Resize:** Images were resized to a predetermined dimension of 512×512 pixels. **(2) Random Horizontal Flip:** Images were randomly flipped horizontally. **(3) Random Vertical Flip:** Images underwent random vertical flips. **(4) Random Rotation:** A random rotation within the range of -180 to $180°$ was applied to the images. **(5) Color Jitter:** Random color variations were introduced to diversify the image data. **(6) Random Adjust Sharpness:** Image sharpness was randomly adjusted during training. **(7) Normalize:** Pixel values were normalized to ensure a consistent range across all images. **(8) Random Erasing:** Approximately 25% of the input images had random portions erased. **(9) Mixup** [21]: A Mixup augmentation technique was also employed to enhance further the model's ability to generalize. It is worth noting that we deliberately omitted the use of Random Crop in our DA strategy. Our observations revealed that Random Crop had the adverse effect of distorting the geometric structures of retinal images while reducing prediction precision.

Training Configuration: Our training configuration encompasses a spectrum of critical hyperparameters and settings that are essential for ensuring the convergence and efficacy of our deep learning model. We employed the AdamP [7] optimizer to optimize the model's parameters throughout the training process, with the initial learning rate set at 0.001. To facilitate swifter convergence, we incorporated a Cosine learning rate scheduler, dynamically adjusting the learning rate during training. The model underwent an extensive training regimen spanning 800 epochs, guaranteeing its ability to capture intricate patterns within the dataset. Additionally, we applied a weight decay of 0.001 to counter overfitting and manage the growth of model parameters. To initiate training smoothly, we introduced a warm-up phase consisting of 20 epochs, gradually increasing the learning rate. This warm-up phase featured a linear learning rate scheduler.

The meticulous selection of data augmentation techniques and finely-tuned training configurations played a pivotal role in elevating our model's performance to remarkable levels, a fact substantiated by the compelling experimental findings meticulously presented in Sect. 4. In Table 1, we provide an exhaustive overview of our comprehensive training configuration, shedding light on the intricate settings that underpin our model's success. Notably, our approach stands as a testament to the power of fundamental techniques and principled methodologies, achieving outstanding performance without reliance on any specialized or esoteric tricks. This reaffirms the robustness and effectiveness of simple baselines in addressing complex tasks.

Table 1. All training configuration.

Data Augmentation	Resize, Random Horizontal Flip, Random Vertical Flip, Random Rotation, ColorJitter, Random Adjust Sharpness, Normalize, Random Erasing Mixup
optimizer	AdamP
Initial Learning Rate	0.001
lr scheduler	Cosine
Epochs	800
Weight decay	0.001
Warmup epoch	20
Warmup lr sheduler	Linear

4 Results

In this section, we present the outcomes of our participation in the competition, with a specific focus on the final challenge rankings based on the official testing set, as detailed in Table 2. We compare our team's performance, referred to as "Ours (Rank 3rd)," to that of the top-ranking teams, "Rank 1st" and "Rank 2nd," using key evaluation metrics, including R-Squared and Mean Absolute Error (MAE). Additionally, we provide insights into the computational efficiency of our approach by examining CPU time utilization.

Model Performance: In the domain of predictive accuracy, our model achieved a commendable R-Squared value of 0.8433 and a Mean Absolute Error (MAE) of 0.7970 on the official testing set. While these metrics position us in the third rank, it is crucial to acknowledge the formidable competition posed by the top two teams, who demonstrated exemplary performance with R-Squared values of 0.8735 (Rank 1st) and 0.8636 (Rank 2nd). The MAE values of the leading teams, 0.7080 (Rank 1st) and 0.7326 (Rank 2nd), further underscore their proficiency in tackling the challenge. We also randomly picked up four images from the validation set to compare the prediction of our method and the ground truth in Fig. 1.

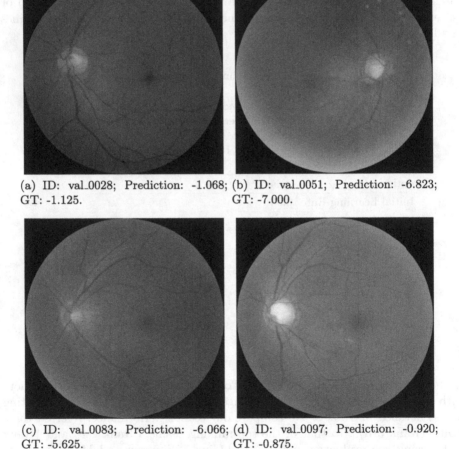

(a) ID: val_0028; Prediction: -1.068; GT: -1.125.

(b) ID: val_0051; Prediction: -6.823; GT: -7.000.

(c) ID: val_0083; Prediction: -6.066; GT: -5.625.

(d) ID: val_0097; Prediction: -0.920; GT: -0.875.

Fig. 1. Comparison between the prediction of our method and the ground truth.

Table 2. Final challenge rank based on official testing set.

Team	R-Squared	Mean Absolute Error	CPU time
Rank 1st	0.8735	0.7080	1.7178
Rank 2nd	0.8636	0.7326	0.9830
Ours (Rank 3rd)	0.8433	0.7970	0.1584

Computational Efficiency: Beyond model performance, we assessed the computational efficiency inherent in our approach, as manifested by the CPU time required for the task. Our method showcased notable efficiency, with a mere CPU time consumption of 0.1584. This efficiency stands in stark contrast to the resource demands of the top-performing teams, with "Rank 1st" utilizing 1.7178 units of CPU time and "Rank 2nd" consuming 0.9830 units. It is worth emphasizing that our model achieved exceptional performance while significantly economizing on CPU time, rendering it an attractive choice for resource-constrained applications.

5   Discussion: The Significance of Proper Data Augmentation

Table 3. Comparing results on validation set with/without random crop data augmentation.

	R-Squared	MAE
w/ randcrop	0.6862	0.9652
w.o randcrop	0.8389	0.6892

This work achieved remarkable results on the *Prediction of Spherical Equivalent* challenge with the Vanilla ResNet. We majorly investigated the critical role of DA in the context of our SE prediction task. As highlighted in Sect. 3, it is notable that we did not include random crop as part of our DA combination. Contrary to some expectations, our experiments demonstrated that introducing random crop had a significant detrimental effect on the model's performance, as depicted in Table 3. This unexpected result underscores the importance of carefully selecting and fine-tuning data augmentation strategies for specific tasks. Data augmentation is a fundamental technique in machine learning, particularly in domains with limited labeled data. It aids in expanding the dataset by generating new, diverse samples through various transformations, thereby enhancing the model's ability to generalize from the available data.

The absence of random crop in our DA combination was a deliberate choice driven by the recognition that not all augmentation techniques are universally beneficial. While the random crop is known to be effective in tasks like image classification, it proved counterproductive for our SE prediction task. The spherical equivalent (SE) can be determined via the following formulae: Optimal subjective spherical component (S) plus half of the subjective cylindrical component (C). Algebraically, the formula is $SE = S + C/2$. We can boldly assume that the random crop potentially ruin the structure competence of the fundus photography. The reduction in model performance suggests that certain transformations may introduce noise or inconsistencies in the data that are detrimental to the learning process. In the case of random crop, it appears to disrupt the critical spatial relationships within our optometric data, ultimately hindering the model's capacity to predict SE values accurately. This outcome underscores the need for a principled approach to data augmentation, one that considers the specific characteristics of the dataset and the nature of the task. Blindly applying a wide range of augmentations without assessing their impact can lead to suboptimal results. It is imperative for the entire community to shift their emphasis towards a deeper understanding and meticulous curation of data, recognizing that the quality and relevance of data play a pivotal role in shaping the success of machine learning endeavors, often more so than the allure of sophisticated models.

6   Conclusion

In this paper, we have delved into the realm of Spherical Equivalent (SE) prediction, demonstrating the remarkable potential of a simple Residual Network (ResNet) architecture, unadorned by intricate techniques or modifications. Our exploration has yielded insights of paramount significance for the field of machine learning and optometry. Through extensive experimentation and analysis, we have shown that the architectural strength of ResNet, with its inherent capacity to capture complex relationships in data, can be harnessed effectively for precise SE estimations. Our model achieved commendable results, holding its own in a fiercely competitive landscape where elaborate methods often dominate. Furthermore, our study underscores the necessity of judiciously tailored data augmentation strategies, emphasizing that not all augmentations are universally advantageous. This critical finding encourages a data-centric approach, urging the community to prioritize a nuanced understanding of data characteristics over the allure of sophisticated models. As we conclude this exploration, we affirm that the confluence of ResNet's architectural elegance and data-centricity represents a promising direction for advancing SE prediction and, by extension, the broader domain of medical applications in machine learning. By steering our focus towards the quality, relevance, and diversity of data, and by appreciating the power of simplicity in architectural choices, we can navigate the intricate landscape of optometry with greater precision, offering enhanced vision correction solutions and contributing to the continued progress of healthcare through machine learning.

References

1. Arega, T.W., Legrand, F., Bricq, S., Meriaudeau, F.: Using MRI-specific data augmentation to enhance the segmentation of right ventricle in multi-disease, multi-center and multi-view cardiac MRI. In: Puyol Anton, E., et al. (eds.) Statistical Atlases and Computational Models of the Heart. Multi-Disease, Multi-View, and Multi-Center Right Ventricular Segmentation in Cardiac MRI Challenge. Lecture Notes in Computer Science(), vol. 13131, pp. 250–258. Springer, Cham (2021). https://doi.org/10.1007/978-3-030-93722-5_27

2. Charng, J., Alam, K., Swartz, G., Kugelman, J., Alonso-Caneiro, D., Mackey, D.A., Chen, F.K.: Deep learning: applications in retinal and optic nerve diseases. Clin. Exp. Optom. **106**(5), 466–475 (2023)

3. Dai, L., Wu, L., Li, H., Cai, C., Wu, Q., Kong, H., Liu, R., Wang, X., Hou, X., Liu, Y., et al.: A deep learning system for detecting diabetic retinopathy across the disease spectrum. Nat. Commun. **12**(1), 3242 (2021)

4. Dosovitskiy, A., et al.: An image is worth 16x16 words: transformers for image recognition at scale. arXiv preprint: arXiv:2010.11929 (2020)

5. Enaholo, E.S., Musa, M.J., Zeppieri, M.: The spherical equivalent. In: StatPearls [Internet]. StatPearls Publishing (2023)

6. He, K., Zhang, X., Ren, S., Sun, J.: Deep residual learning for image recognition. In: Proceedings of the IEEE Conference on Computer Vision and Pattern Recognition. pp. 770–778 (2016)

7. Heo, B., et al.: AdamP: slowing down the slowdown for momentum optimizers on scale-invariant weights. arXiv preprint: arXiv:2006.08217 (2020)

8. Holden, B.A., et al.: Global prevalence of myopia and high myopia and temporal trends from 2000 through 2050. Ophthalmology **123**(5), 1036–1042 (2016)

9. Ikuno, Y.: Overview of the complications of high myopia. Retina **37**(12), 2347–2351 (2017)

10. Li, X., Hu, X., Yu, L., Zhu, L., Fu, C.W., Heng, P.A.: CANet: cross-disease attention network for joint diabetic retinopathy and diabetic macular edema grading. IEEE Trans. Med. Imaging **39**, 1483–1493 (2020)

11. Liu, R., et al.: DeepDRiD: diabetic retinopathy-grading and image quality estimation challenge. Patterns **3**(6) (2022)

12. Liu, Z., et al.: A convnet for the 2020s. In: Proceedings of the IEEE/CVF Conference on Computer Vision and Pattern Recognition, pp. 11976–11986 (2022)

13. Ohno-Matsui, K., et al.: International photographic classification and grading system for myopic maculopathy. Am. J. Ophthalmol. **159**(5), 877–883 (2015)

14. Silva, R.: Myopic maculopathy: a review. Ophthalmologica **228**(4), 197–213 (2012)

15. Singh, A., Jothi Balaji, J., Rasheed, M.A., Jayakumar, V., Raman, R., Lakshminarayanan, V.: Evaluation of explainable deep learning methods for ophthalmic diagnosis. Clin. Ophthalmol., 2573–2581 (2021)

16. Sun, R., Li, Y., Zhang, T., Mao, Z., Wu, F., Zhang, Y.: Lesion-aware transformers for diabetic retinopathy grading. In: Proceedings of the IEEE/CVF Conference on Computer Vision and Pattern Recognition, pp. 10938–10947 (2021)

17. Uysal, E.S., Bilici, M.Ş., Zaza, B.S., Özgenç, M.Y., Boyar, O.: Exploring the limits of data augmentation for retinal vessel segmentation. arXiv preprint: arXiv:2105.09365 (2021)

18. Wang, Z., Yin, Y., Shi, J., Fang, W., Li, H., Wang, X.: Zoom-in-Net: deep mining lesions for diabetic retinopathy detection. In: Descoteaux, M., Maier-Hein, L.,

Franz, A., Jannin, P., Collins, D., Duchesne, S. (eds.) Medical Image Computing and Computer Assisted Intervention – MICCAI 2017. Lecture Notes in Computer Science(), vol. 10435, pp. 267–275. Springer, Cham (2017). https://doi.org/10.1007/978-3-319-66179-7_31

19. Yokoi, T., Ohno-Matsui, K.: Diagnosis and treatment of myopic maculopathy. Asia-Pac. J. Ophthalmol. **7**(6), 415–421 (2018)

20. Yu, S., et al.: MIL-VT: multiple instance learning enhanced vision transformer for fundus image classification. In: de Bruijne, M., et al. (eds.) Medical Image Computing and Computer Assisted Intervention - MICCAI 2021. Lecture Notes in Computer Science(), vol. 12908, pp. 45–54. Springer, Cham (2021). https://doi.org/10.1007/978-3-030-87237-3_5

21. Zhang, H., Cisse, M., Dauphin, Y.N., Lopez-Paz, D.: mixup: beyond empirical risk minimization. arXiv preprint: arXiv:1710.09412 (2017)

22. Zhou, Y., et al.: Collaborative learning of semi-supervised segmentation and classification for medical images. In: Proceedings of the IEEE/CVF Conference on Computer Vision and Pattern Recognition (2019)

23. Zhu, W., et al.: Self-supervised equivariant regularization reconciles multiple instance learning: Joint referable diabetic retinopathy classification and lesion segmentation. In: 18th International Symposium on Medical Information Processing and Analysis (SIPAIM) (2022)

24. Zhu, W., et al.: OTRE: where optimal transport guided unpaired image-to-image translation meets regularization by enhancing. In: Frangi, A., de Bruijne, M., Wassermann, D., Navab, N. (eds.) Information Processing in Medical Imaging. Lecture Notes in Computer Science, vol. 13939, pp. 415–427. Springer, Cham (2023). https://doi.org/10.1007/978-3-031-34048-2_32

25. Zhu, W., Qiu, P., Farazi, M., Nandakumar, K., Dumitrascu, O.M., Wang, Y.: Optimal transport guided unsupervised learning for enhancing low-quality retinal images. arXiv preprint: arXiv:2302.02991 (2023)

26. Zhu, W., Qiu, P., Lepore, N., Dumitrascu, O.M., Wang, Y.: NNMobile-Net: rethinking CNN design for deep learning-based retinopathy research. arXiv preprint: arXiv:2306.01289 (2023)

Semi-supervised Learning for Myopic Maculopathy Analysis

Jónathan Heras(✉) 🆔

Department of Mathematics and Computer Science, Universidad de La Rioja,
Logroño, Spain
jonathan.heras@unirioja.es

Abstract. Myopia is a common ocular disease that affects large populations in the world. This disease can lead to visual impairment due to the development of different types of myopic maculopathy. Therefore, prompt screening and intervention are necessary to prevent the further progression of myopic maculopathy to avoid vision loss. However, the manual inspection process is a time-consuming task that relies heavily on the experience of ophthalmologists. Towards advancing the state-of-the-art in automatic myopic maculopathy analysis using retinal fundus images, the "Myopic Maculopathy Analysis Challenge (MMAC) 2023" was launched. In this work, we present how semi-supervised learning methods can be applied to tackle two of the tasks proposed in the MMAC challenge: the segmentation of myopic maculopathy plus lesions, and the prediction of spherical equivalent. In particular, we have applied a pseudo-labeling approach for the segmentation task obtaining an average Dice similarity score of 0.6706, and a data-distillation procedure for the regression problem obtaining an R-square score of 0.7906. In both cases, we used the data from the other tasks of the challenge to increase the size of the original dataset with an automatically annotated dataset. This approach obtained the fourth position in both the segmentation and spherical equivalent prediction tasks.

Keywords: Semi-Supervised Learning · Myopic Maculopathy · Segmentation · Regression

1 Introduction

Myopia is a common ocular disease that affects large populations in the world [9]. In the worst cases, myopia might lead to visual impairment [29] due to the development of different types of myopic maculopathy [13,20]. According to the severity, myopic maculopathy can be classified into five categories: no macular lesions, tessellated fundus, diffuse chorioretinal atrophy, patchy chorioretinal atrophy and macular atrophy [17]. In addition, three additional "Plus" lesions are also defined and added to these categories: lacquer cracks (LC), choroidal neovascularization (CNV), and Fuchs spot (FS). Myopic maculopathy is likely

This work was partially supported by Grant PID2020-115225RB-I00 funded by MCIN/AEI/10.13039/501100011033.

B. Sheng et al. (Eds.): MICCAI 2023, LNCS 14563, pp. 75–82, 2024.
https://doi.org/10.1007/978-3-031-54857-4_7

to progress more quickly after the stage of tessellated fundus [20]. Moreover, higher degrees of myopia are associated with an increased risk of severe types of myopic maculopathy, so the prediction of spherical equivalent can help diagnose the risk of macular maculopathy.

Prompt screening and intervention are necessary to prevent the further progression of myopic maculopathy to avoid vision loss. However, the myopic maculopathy diagnosis is limited by the manual inspection process of image by image, which is time-consuming and relies heavily on the experience of ophthalmologists. Therefore, an effective computer-aided system is essential to help ophthalmologists analyze myopic maculopathy, further providing accurate diagnosis and reasonable intervention for this disease. In this context, the "Myopic Maculopathy Analysis Challenge 2023" (MMAC challenge) aims to advance the state-of-the-art in automatic myopic maculopathy analysis using retinal fundus images. The challenge consists of three tasks: (1) classification of myopic maculopathy, (2) segmentation of myopic maculopathy plus lesions, and (3) prediction of spherical equivalent.

In this paper, we present our approach to tackle Tasks 2 and 3 using semi-supervised learning methods [24]. The rest of the paper is organised as follows. In the next section, we present a literature review of works related to automatically detecting myopic maculopathy. After that, we provide an overview of the datasets provided in the MMAC challenge. Subsequently, we present our approach for the automatic segmentation of myopic maculopathy plus lesions and the obtained results. Then, we introduce the method applied for estimating spherical equivalence and the obtained results. Finally, we end the paper with some conclusions. All the code associated with this paper is available at https:// github.com/joheras/mmac.

2   Related Work

Deep Learning methods have become the by-default approach for automatically diagnosing retinal diseases such as Diabetic Retinopathy [4,15], Glaucoma [5], Age-Related Macular Degeneration [7], or Epiretinal Membrane [2] among others. In the case of myopic maculopathy, we can find in the literature several automatic systems for diagnosing this disease [6,8,26]. However, the number of works that are focused on the segmentation of myopic maculopathy plus lesions, and the prediction of spherical equivalent is scarce.

In the segmentation case, Deep Learning methods have been widely employed to segment retinal structures including optic disk, optic cup, arteries, vein, or retinal vessel [14]. However, as far as we are aware, the automatic segmentation of structures related to myopic maculopathy has not been studied yet.

Finally, for the prediction of spherical equivalent, we can find in the literature several works that estimate this feature by using historical data [11]. Using retinal fundus images, Varadarajan et al. [25] built a model based on ResNet that achieved a mean absolute error (MAE) of 0.91 diopters in the AREDS dataset; Shi et al. [19] proposed a MDNet model that achieved a MAE of 1.1150 in a dataset from China Aier Eye Hospital and Southern Medical University; and, Xu et al. [28] combined a Convolutional Neural Network with a Recurrent Neural Network to reach a MAE of 0.1740 diopters.

3   Datasets

The dataset provided for the MMAC challenge consists of retinal fundus images from two data centers, and for the three different tasks. For each task, the dataset is split into three groups: training, validation, and test; see the statistics for each dataset in Table 1. The training images together with their annotation were publicly released, whereas both the validation and test sets were not publicly released but participants of the challenge had to submit their models through the CodaLab platform to obtain the results — if the submission was successful, the results for the validation set were shown, but not for the test set. Patient metadata were also provided for each task, including age, sex, height (in centimetres, cm), and weight (in kilograms, kg); however, since some metadata might be missing, we did not consider it for our methods.

Table 1. Statistics of the MMAC datasets.

	Task 1	Task2			Task 3
		LC	CNV	FS	
Training set	1143	63	32	54	992
Validation set	248	12	7	13	205
Test set	915	46	22	45	806

For each task, the best results on the test set was used for ranking. The metrics used for ranking the submissions of Tasks 2 and 3, that are the ones considered in this paper, are as follows. For Task 2, the Dice similarity coefficient (DSC) was calculated for each class independently and then results were averaged for the final ranking. In case of a tie, the recall and precision was used for auxiliary ranking. For Task 3, rankings were computed based on the R-squared and mean absolute errors computed on all test cases.

4   Segmentation of Myopic Maculopathy Plus Lesions

We handled the segmentation of LC, CNV, and FS following the semi-supervised learning method presented in [1]. This method is called pseudo-labeling is diagrammatically depicted in Fig. 1. Namely, for each one of the lesions, we proceed as follows. First of all, from the annotated dataset of Task 2, we trained a segmentation model using the DeepLabV3 architecture with a ResNet 50 backbone [3]. Then, we annotated the images of the datasets provided for Tasks 1 and 3 of the challenge by obtaining their segmentation using the trained model. As a third step, we combined the original dataset of Task 2 and the semi-supervised dataset generated in the previous stage. Subsequently, from such a combined dataset, we trained three models using the DeepLabV3 architecture with a ResNet 50 backbone, the DeepLabV3 architecture with an EfficientNet B3 backbone, and the Unet++ architecture with a ResNet 50 backbone [30]. Finally, in order to obtain the predictions for new images, the three models trained in the previous step were ensembled by averaging their predictions. The architectures with their respective backbones were implemented in PyTorch using the Segmentation models library [12] and have been trained thanks to the functionality of the FastAI library [10] on an Nvidia RTX 3090 Ti GPU.

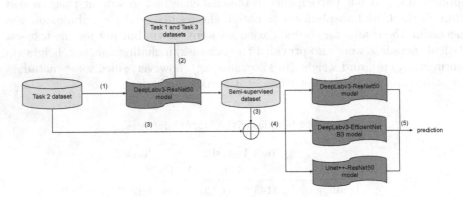

Fig. 1. Semi-supervised learning procedure for Task 2.

An ablation study of the results obtained with the proposed approach evaluated in the test set is provided in Table 2. If we observe the average Dice similarity coefficient, there is a natural increment of such value when we compose the different elements of our method. Namely, the worst results were obtained when using only the dataset from Task 2; then, the results improved when we applied pseudo-labeling and trained new models with the combined version of the dataset; and, finally, the ensemble of models produced the best results. This progression also occurs if we inspect the results for the CNV and FS lesions; however, for the LC segmentation models, the only model that obtains better results after applying pseudo-labeling is the Unet++-Resnet50 model. Note that this approach is quite time-consuming since it requires the ensemble of several models; hence, if we were interested in reducing that burden, the best option would be to use the Unet++ model with a ResNet 50 backbone for segmenting LC lesions, and the DeepLabv3+ models with an EfficientNet B3 backbone to segment CNV and FS lesions. Some examples of the predicted lesions using our best approach are presented in Fig. 2.

Table 2. Ablation study of the different components of the segmentation method. SS stands for Semi-Supervised Learning.

	LC DSC	CNV DSC	FS DSC	Avg DSC	Avg Recall	Avg Precision
DeepLabv3-Resnet50	0.6519	0.4231	0.7111	0.5945	0.6443	0.6532
DeepLabv3-Resnet50 SS	0.6394	0.4344	0.7343	0.6027	0.6555	0.6392
DeepLabv3-EfficientNetB3 SS	0.6174	0.5606	0.7742	0.6507	0.6893	0.6837
Unet++-Resnet50 SS	0.6640	0.4238	0.7461	0.6113	0.6748	0.6434
Ensemble	0.6641	0.5793	0.7684	0.6706	0.7560	0.6769

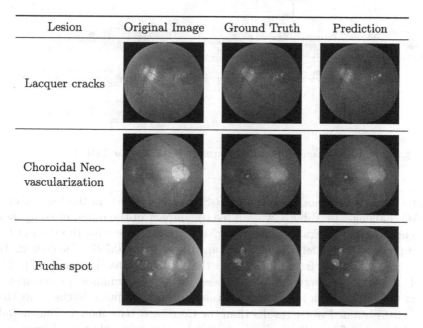

Fig. 2. Samples of the predictions produced by our segmentation approach.

5   Prediction of Spherical Equivalent

We handled the estimation of spherical equivalent using a data distillation approach [18], see Fig. 3. First of all, from the annotated dataset of Task 3, we trained a regression model using the ConvNext architecture [16]. Then, we annotated the images of the datasets provided for Tasks 1 and 2 of the challenge by applying Test Time Augmentation (TTA) [21] using the ConvNext model; that is, given an image, we created random modifications of such an image, performed predictions on them using the model, and, finally, returned the average of those predictions. As a third step, we combined the original dataset of Task 3 and the semi-supervised dataset generated in the previous stage. Subsequently, from such a combined dataset, we trained three models using the ConvNext architecture, the EfficientNet v2 architecture [22], and the ConvMixer architecture [23]. Finally, in order to obtain the prediction for new images, we applied TTA to the three models trained in the previous step using both horizontal and vertical flips, and finally averaged their predictions. The architectures with their respective backbones were implemented in PyTorch using the Timm library [27] and have been trained thanks to the functionality of the FastAI library [10] on an Nvidia RTX 3090 Ti GPU.

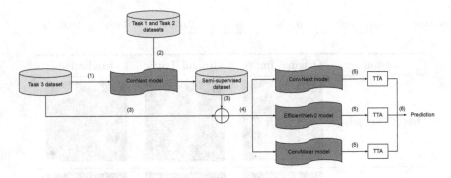

Fig. 3. Semi-supervised learning procedure for Task 3

The proposed method achieved an R-Squared of 0.7906 in the test set of the MMAC challenge. In Table 3, we can see the impact of the different components of the approach. Just training the ConvNext architecture with the dataset from Task 3 produced a model that achieved an R-Squared of 0.727. The combination of the original dataset from Task 3 with the semi-supervised dataset helped the models to generalize better as can be seen in the performance improvement of models trained on such a combined dataset — the exception is the ConvMixer model that obtained worse results than the ConvNext base model. The ensemble of models outperforms the individual models, indicating that combining models with diverse approaches can lead to improved overall performance. Finally, applying TTA to the ensemble of models further boosted the performance of our approach.

Table 3. Ablation study of the different components of the regression method. SS stands for Semi-Supervised Learning.

	R-Squared ↑	MAE ↓
ConvNext	0.7270	1.0335
ConvNext SS	0.7705	0.9720
ConvMixer SS	0.7076	1.0676
EfficientNet v2 SS	0.7512	1.0763
Ensemble	0.7823	0.9486
Ensemble + TTA	0.7906	0.9427

6 Conclusions

In this work, we have shown how semi-supervised learning methods can be employed to improve the performance of models for segmenting myopic maculopathy lesions and for predicting spherical equivalence from retinal fundus images. Hence, the semi-supervised learning approaches reduce the burden of annotating images, and produce competitive results.

References

1. Casado-García, A., Heras, J., Milella, A., Marani, R.: Semi-supervised deep learning and low-cost cameras for the semantic segmentation of natural images in viticulture. Precision Agric. **23**(6), 2001–2026 (2022)
2. Casado-García, Á., et al.: Prediction of epiretinal membrane from retinal fundus images using deep learning. In: Alba, E., et al. (eds.) Advances in Artificial Intelligence. Lecture Notes in Computer Science(), vol. 12882, pp. 3–13. Springer, Cham (2021). https://doi.org/10.1007/978-3-030-85713-4_1
3. Chen, L.C., Zhu, Y., Papandreou, G., Schroff, F., Adam, H.: Encoder-decoder with Atrous separable convolution for semantic image segmentation. In: Ferrari, V., Hebert, M., Sminchisescu, C., Weiss, Y. (eds.) Computer Vision - ECCV 2018. Lecture Notes in Computer Science(), vol. 11211, pp. 801–818. Springer, Cham (2018). https://doi.org/10.1007/978-3-030-01234-2_49
4. Dai, L., et al.: A deep learning system for detecting diabetic retinopathy across the disease spectrum. Nat. Commun. **12**(1), 3242 (2021)
5. De Vente, C., et al.: AIROGS: artificial intelligence for robust glaucoma screening challenge. IEEE Trans. Med. Imaging (2023)
6. Devda, J., Eswari, R.: Pathological myopia image analysis using deep learning. Procedia Comput. Sci. **165**, 239–244 (2019)
7. Domínguez, C., et al.: Binary and multi-class automated detection of age-related macular degeneration using convolutional-and transformer-based architectures. Comput. Methods Programs Biomed. **229**, 107302 (2023)
8. Du, R., et al.: Deep learning approach for automated detection of myopic maculopathy and pathologic myopia in fundus images. Ophthalmol. Retina **5**(12), 1235–1244 (2021)
9. Holden, B.A., et al.: Global prevalence of myopia and high myopia and temporal trends from 2000 through 2050. Ophthalmology **123**(5), 1036–1042 (2016)

10. Howard, J., Gugger, S., Chintala, S.: Deep Learning for Coders with Fastai and PyTorch: AI Applications Without a PhD. O'Reilly Media, Incorporated, Sebastopol (2020)
11. Huang, J., et al.: Myopia prediction for children and adolescents via time-aware deep learning. Sci. Rep. **13**(1), 5430 (2023)
12. Iakubovskii, P.: Segmentation models PyTorch (2019). https://github.com/qubvel/segmentation_models.pytorch
13. Ikuno, Y.: Overview of the complications of high myopia. Retina **37**(12), 2347–2351 (2017)
14. Ilesanmi, A.E., Ilesanmi, T., Gbotoso, A.G.: A systematic review of retinal fundus image segmentation and classification methods using convolutional neural networks. Healthcare Analytics, 100261 (2023)
15. Liu, R., et al.: DeepDRiD: diabetic retinopathy-grading and image quality estimation challenge. Patterns **3**(6) (2022)
16. Liu, Z., et al.: A convnet for the 2020s. In: Proceedings of the IEEE/CVF Conference on Computer Vision and Pattern Recognition, pp. 11976–11986 (2022)
17. Ohno-Matsui, K., et al.: International photographic classification and grading system for myopic maculopathy. Am. J. Ophthalmol. **159**(5), 877–883 (2015)
18. Radosavovic, I., et al.: Data distillation: towards omni-supervised learning. In: Proceedings of the IEEE Conference on Computer Vision and Pattern Recognition, pp. 4119–4128 (2018)
19. Shi, Z., et al.: A method for the automatic detection of myopia in Optos fundus images based on deep learning. Int. J. Numer. Methods Biomed. Eng. **37**(6), e3460 (2021)
20. Silva, R.: Myopic maculopathy: a review. Ophthalmologica **228**(4), 197–213 (2012)
21. Simonyan, K., Zisserman, A.: Very deep convolutional networks for large-scale image recognition. In: International Conference on Learning Representations (2015)
22. Tan, M., Le, Q.: Efficientnetv2: smaller models and faster training. In: International Conference on Machine Learning, pp. 10096–10106. PMLR (2021)
23. Trockman, A., Kolter, J.Z.: Patches are all you need? arXiv preprint: arXiv:2201.09792 (2022)
24. Van Engelen, J.E., Hoos, H.H.: A survey on semi-supervised learning. Mach. Learn. **109**(2), 373–440 (2020)
25. Varadarajan, A.V., et al.: Deep learning for predicting refractive error from retinal fundus images. Invest. Ophthalmol. Vis. Sci. **59**(7), 2861–2868 (2018)
26. Wang, R., et al.: Efficacy of a deep learning system for screening myopic maculopathy based on color fundus photographs. Ophthalmol Therapy **12**(1), 469–484 (2023)
27. Wightman, R.: PyTorch image models (2019). https://github.com/rwightman/pytorch-image-models. https://doi.org/10.5281/zenodo.4414861
28. Xu, D., et al.: Deep learning for predicting refractive error from multiple photorefraction images. Biomed. Eng. Online **21**(1), 1–14 (2022)
29. Yokoi, T., Ohno-Matsui, K.: Diagnosis and treatment of myopic maculopathy. Asia-Pac. J. Ophthalmol. **7**(6), 415–421 (2018)
30. Zhou, Z., et al.: UNet++: a nested u-net architecture for medical image segmentation. In: Stoyanov, D., et al. (eds.) Deep Learning in Medical Image Analysis and Multimodal Learning for Clinical Decision Support. Lecture Notes in Computer Science(), vol. 11045, pp. 3–11. Springer, Cham (2018). https://doi.org/10.1007/978-3-030-00889-5_1

A Clinically Guided Approach for Training Deep Neural Networks for Myopic Maculopathy Classification

Fabian Yii[1,2]([envelope]) [iD]

[1] Centre for Clinical Brain Sciences, The University of Edinburgh, Edinburgh, UK
fabian.yii@ed.ac.uk
[2] Curle Ophthalmology Laboratory, The University of Edinburgh, Edinburgh, UK

Abstract. Pathologic myopia (PM) is a sight-threatening disease characterised by abnormal ocular changes due to excessive axial elongation in myopes. One important clinical manifestation of PM is myopic maculopathy (MM), which is categorised into 5 ordinal classes based on the established META-PM classification framework. This paper details a robust deep learning approach to automatically classifying MM from colour fundus photographs as part of the recently held Myopic Maculopathy Analysis Challenge (MMAC). A ResNet-18 model pretrained on ImageNet-1K was trained for the task. Pertinent MM lesions (patchy or macular atrophy) were manually segmented in images from the MMAC dataset and another publicly available dataset (PALM) to create a collection of lesion masks based on which an additional 250 images with severe MM were synthesised to mitigate class imbalance in the original training set. The image synthesis pipeline was guided by clinical domain knowledge: (1) synthesised macular atrophy tended to be circular with a regressed fibrovascular membrane near its centre, while patchy atrophy was more irregular and varied more greatly in size; (2) synthesised images were created using images with diffuse or patchy atrophy as background; and (3) synthesised images included examples that were not easily classifiable (e.g. creating patchy lesions that were in close proximity to the fovea). This, coupled with mix-up augmentation and ensemble prediction via test-time augmentation, enabled the model to rank first in the validation phase and fifth in the test phase. The source code is freely available at https://github.com/fyii200/MyopicMaculopathyClassification.

Keywords: deep learning · myopic maculopathy · pathologic myopia · META-PM · clinical domain knowledge

1 Introduction

Myopia (or short-sightedness) is associated with excessive axial length (i.e. distance from the anterior corneal surface to the retina at the posterior pole) and a wide range of structural changes in the posterior segment of the eye [1]. These changes are thought

F. Yii is supported by the Medical Research Council [grant number MR/N013166/1]. The funder had no role in the design and conduct of this work nor the decision to submit this manuscript for publication.

to predispose the eye to various sight-threatening conditions, most notably pathologic myopia (PM), a leading cause of irreversible blindness among adults in parts of the world [2]. One important clinical manifestation of PM is myopic maculopathy (MM), which is a form of macular degeneration (for which effective treatment is not currently available) characterised by progressive central vision loss [2]. Under the established META-PM classification framework [3], MM is categorised into 5 ordinal classes (with increasing severity): normal (category 0), fundus tessellation (category 1), diffuse chorioretinal atrophy (category 2), patchy chorioretinal atrophy (category 3) and macular atrophy (category 4). PM is defined as the presence of MM category 2 or above, or the presence of any "plus" lesions (so called because they can coexist with any MM category) including lacquer cracks, myopic choroidal neovascularisation (mCNV) and Fuchs spot [3].

Previous studies applying deep learning (DL) for PM classification almost invariably treated the task as a binary classification problem, focussing on detecting the presence of PM/MM based on colour fundus photographs [4–11] or optical coherence tomography scans [12]. For instance, Li et al. [4] trained a DL model on over 30,000 fundus photographs using a dual-stream approach that took both the original image and its corresponding histogram-equalised image as input. They reported an area under the receiver operating characteristic curve (AUC) of 0.998 and 0.994 on two different external test sets. Despite good test performance reported by the studies cited above, binary classification is ultimately of limited clinical value because it does not differentiate between eyes with different disease severities and manifestations. A small number of studies, though, sought to perform multiclass classification of PM/MM [13–16]. For example, Du et al.[14] used an ensemble learning approach in which four DL-based binary classifiers were trained to detect different MM categories. They reported an AUC of 0.970, 0.978, 0.982 and 0.881 for MM category 2, MM category 3, MM category 4 and mCNV, respectively. However, none of the datasets used for model development in the existing literature is publicly available, thus precluding meaningful comparison or benchmarking of DL models for PM/MM classification.

The Myopic Maculopathy Analysis Challenge (MMAC) held in conjunction with MICCAI 2023 addressed these limitations by providing the first publicly and freely available benchmark dataset with fine-grained MM labels for classification model development. This paper details a clinically guided approach to training DL models to automatically classify MM from colour fundus photographs, which enabled the final model to rank first and fifth in the validation phase and test phase of the challenge, respectively. It was shown that: (1) image synthesis guided by clinical domain knowledge to generate new training examples with severe MM could improve model robustness to imbalanced class distribution; and (2) existing "tricks" such as test-time augmentation were simple yet effective in improving classification performance. The source code is freely available at https://github.com/fyii200/MyopicMaculopathyClassification.

2 Methods

2.1 Datasets and Pre-processing

The MMAC dataset comprised 2306 macula-centred colour fundus photographs (800 × 800 pixels) with ground-truth labels per the META-PM classification framework (5 classes) described above. Of these images, 1143, 248 and 915 were prescribed as training, validation and test images, respectively. The images were taken from patients seen at Shanghai Sixth People's Hospital as part of a myopia screening programme. Ground-truth labels were provided by two ophthalmologists with at least 5 years of experience (quadratic weighted kappa score > 0.85), who graded each image independently and involved a third senior ophthalmologist (>10 years of experience) as the adjudicator in the event of disagreement. The mean ± SD age and spherical equivalent refraction (SER) of the training set were 53.8 ± 10.5 (29 to 93) years and -1.60 ± 2.56 (2.88 to -10.00) D, respectively. Note that the summary statistics for SER were inferred from the training set provided for another task of the challenge (*Task 3*), which focussed on SER prediction and used a sample that was not completely identical (but broadly similar) to the sample used for the present task (i.e. MM classification).

The Pathologic Myopia Challenge (PALM) dataset, which is publicly available and has been described elsewhere [17], was additionally used for model training. The dataset contained 1200 predominantly macula-centred colour fundus photographs (2124 × 2056 or 1444 × 1444 pixels) taken from patients seen at Zhongshan Ophthalmic Center in China, with binary ground-truth labels related to the present task (i.e. PM or no PM). The author (with a background in optometry) regraded the images and converted their corresponding binary labels into more fine-grained labels per the META-PM framework. Sixty-nine images were removed because adequate assessment of the entire macula was impossible due to retinal detachment or poor image quality (severe underexposure), or because a significant area of the macula was not captured (often seen in laterally displaced optic disc-centred photos). Images in both datasets were resized to 512 × 512 pixels and normalised to 0–1 range.

2.2 Image Synthesis Pipeline Guided by Clinical Domain Knowledge

To alleviate the problem of class imbalance in the MMAC (i.e. only 5% had patchy atrophy and 4% had macular atrophy) and PALM (i.e. 13% had patchy atrophy and 14% had macular atrophy) datasets, additional training images with patchy/macular atrophy were synthesised. To achieve this, a lesion bank was first created by segmenting pertinent lesions in (category 3 or 4) images from both datasets via freehand tracing using MATLAB's Image Segmenter app (MathWorks, Inc., Natick, MA, USA; https://uk.mathworks.com/help/images/ref/imagesegmenter-app.html). Lesion segmentation was guided by the knowledge that patchy lesion tended to be more irregular in shape and differed more greatly in size/number/location, while macular atrophy was more likely to be circular with a regressed fibrovascular member near its centre [3]. When segmenting patchy lesion(s), the author capitalised on this domain knowledge by *not* necessarily following the original outline and was at liberty to decide the number of lesions (if more than one) to be segmented in each image to increase the overall data diversity in the training set (i.e. avoid exact replication of the original lesion).

To synthesise (Figs. 1 and 2) an image corresponding to a given MM category, a lesion mask of that category was randomly sampled and fused with a background image (randomly sampled from the MMAC dataset) through linear interpolation. A Gaussian blur filter was applied to the lesion mask to smooth the border between the pasted lesion and background image. Considering that patchy/macular atrophy is characterised by well-defined borders [3], the standard deviation of the Gaussian function (defining the blur filter) was optimised on a case-by-case basis to ensure that an excessive amount of blur was not inadvertently introduced during interpolation. To further increase data diversity, random rotation (up to ± 90°) was applied to the lesion mask. The author ensured that the pasted lesion did not encroach on the fovea when synthesising images with patchy atrophy (category 3), but it was always made to centre on (or displace slightly from) the fovea when synthesising images with macular atrophy (category 4). Background images were always sampled from eyes with either diffuse or patchy atrophy because more severe MM is a known risk factor for disease progression [18].

Of note, the synthesised images included hand-crafted examples with challenging clinical presentations, carefully curated to increase model robustness to cases that were not easily classifiable. For instance, when synthesising a category 3 image, the lesion(s) was occasionally moved very close to (but sparing) the central macula (top panel of Fig. 1). The image synthesis pipeline generated one image at a time, and the decision to include or discard a given synthesised image was made concurrently, until 250 images were finally synthesised (i.e. 125 each for categories 3 and 4; of which, 50% utilised PALM lesion masks). The frequency of each MM category in the final training set is shown in Table 1.

2.3 Mix-Up Augmentation

In addition to regular data augmentations (i.e. random horizontal flip, rotation up to ± 30°, brightness/saturation jitter), mix-up augmentation was applied during training. Mix-up augmentation is an effective, domain-agnostic regularisation technique that generates a new training example by linearly combining a randomly sampled pair of training images along with their labels [19]. It is conceivably useful when the labels are ordinal (as is the case with MM) where "in-between" labels are clinically meaningful (i.e. MM severity can be meaningfully placed on a continuum). To illustrate, a fundus with extensive diffuse atrophy may be more realistically classed as somewhere between MM category 2 and 3 if the lesions are not very well demarcated but characterised by some localised areas of pronounced chorioretinal atrophy. In mix-up augmentation, the degree of linear combination is determined by a parameter called λ (ranges from 0 to 1), which is randomly sampled from a symmetric beta distribution (Fig. 3). In this work, the alpha and beta parameters (of the symmetric beta distribution) were set to 0.4 because it was found to give the best validation performance:

$$\tilde{x} = \lambda \bullet x_i + (1 - \lambda) \bullet x_j \tag{1}$$

$$\tilde{y} = \lambda \bullet y_i + (1 - \lambda) \bullet y_j \tag{2}$$

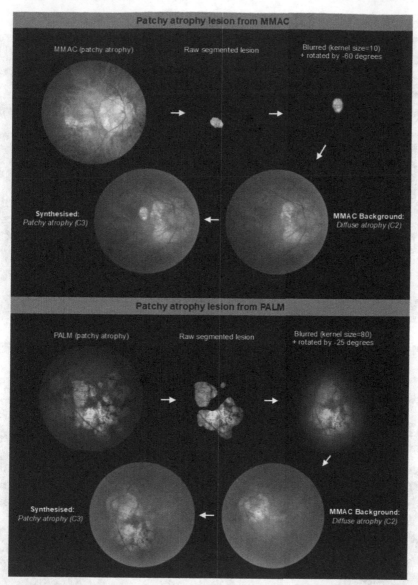

Fig. 1. Visual representation of the pipeline used to synthesise new training examples with patchy atrophy (MM category 3). Top: linear interpolation between a background MMAC image (with diffuse atrophy) and a small patchy lesion derived from an MMAC image. The lesion is deliberately placed in close proximity to central macula (but sparing the fovea) to create a training example that is not easily classifiable. Bottom: linear interpolation between a background MMAC image (with diffuse atrophy) and large patchy lesions derived from a PALM image. A gaussian filter with a larger kernel size is used to make the lesions blend better into the background image. Note that an appropriate degree of rotation and horizontal/vertical shift are applied to the lesion mask to ensure that the retinal vasculature of the pasted lesion match that of the background image.

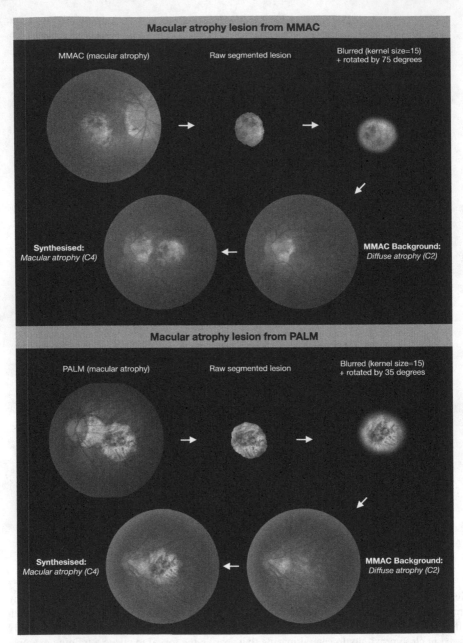

Fig. 2. Visual representation of the pipeline used to synthesise new training examples with macular atrophy (MM category 4): linear interpolation between a background MMAC image (with diffuse atrophy) and a macular atrophy lesion derived from an MMAC (top) or PALM (bottom) image. Note that the lesion, often characterised by the presence of a regressed fibrovascular membrane (seen as a black patch near the centre of the lesion), is made to centre roughly on the fovea. (Color figure online)

Table 1. Frequency of each myopic maculopathy category by dataset.

Category	0	1	2	3	4
MMAC	404	412	224	60	43
PALM	349	261	214	152	155
Synthesised	NA	NA	NA	125	125
Combined	*753*	*673*	*438*	*337*	*323*

where $\tilde{x}$ and $\tilde{y}$ denote the new image and label, respectively, formed by a linear combination of two existing training instances represented by the subscripts i and j.

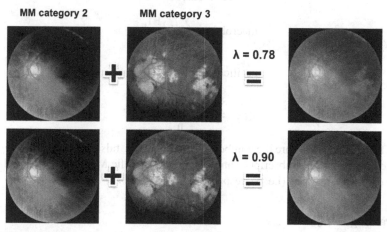

Fig. 3. Mix-up augmentation with a λ value of 0.78 (i.e. 78% MM category 2 + 22% MM category 3) and 0.90 (i.e. 90% MM category 2 + 10% MM category 3); MM: myopic maculopathy.

A variant of Eq. (2) was implemented in this work (i.e. mixing training losses instead of training labels) [20]:

$$\tilde{L} = \lambda \bullet CE(pred, y_i) + (1 - \lambda) \bullet CE(pred, y_i) \tag{3}$$

where CE represents the cross-entropy loss function, $pred$ refers to the model prediction and $\tilde{L}$ denotes the new training loss. In each iteration, mix-up augmentation was applied to the entire batch of images with a probability of 0.5 (i.e. either applied to all images in a given batch or not applied at all). Regular augmentations were only applied after mix-up augmentation to avoid mixing up images that had been rotated differently.

2.4 Evaluation Metrics

Quadratic weighted Cohen's Kappa (Qk), macro-averaged F1 score (macro F1) and macro-averaged specificity (MS) were used as the main evaluation metrics. Hyperparameter tuning and model selection were based on the mean of these metrics computed on the validation set (with Qk as the tiebreaker). Cohen's Kappa [21, 22] is a popular metric for multiclass classification, and the quadratic weighted variant (i.e. penalty due to misclassification increases quadratically as prediction moves further away from the actual class) is particularly suited for MM classification because visual acuity is known to reduce non-linearly with increasing MM severity [23]. Qk is defined as:

$$Qk = \frac{P_o - P_e}{1 - P_e} \tag{4}$$

where P_o and P_e denote the (quadratic weighted) probability of agreement and probability of expected agreement. The formulas for macro F1 and MS are as follows:

$$F1_c = \frac{TP}{TP + 0.5(FP + FN)} \tag{5}$$

$$macroF1 = \frac{\sum_{i=1}^{n} F1_c}{n} \tag{6}$$

$$specificity_c = \frac{TN}{TN + FP} \tag{7}$$

$$MS = \frac{\sum_{i=1}^{n} specificity_c}{n} \tag{8}$$

where TP, FP, TN and FN are the number of true positives, false positives, true negatives and false negatives. The subscripts c and n denote a specific MM category and the total number of MM categories (i.e. 5), respectively.

2.5 Training Details

A vanilla ResNet-18 pre-trained on the ImageNet-1K dataset was trained for 50 epochs using a batch size of 20. Other deeper architectures including ResNet-34, ResNet-50 and ResNet-101 were also explored, but none of them yielded a practically important improvement over ResNet-18. ADAM optimizer (initial learning rate: 5e-5; weight decay: 5e-4) was used with a cosine annealing scheduler. A weighted cross-entropy loss function with 0.1 label smoothing [24] was used, where the weight of a given class was computed by taking the ratio of the total number of images (across classes) to the number of images of that class (i.e. weights were 0.67, 0.75, 1.15, 1.51 and 1.57 for MM category 0 to 4). The official PyTorch framework in Python (version 3.10.9; https://www.python.org/) was used, and all experiments were conducted using a NVIDIA RTX A5000 24GB GPU.

2.6 Ensemble Prediction via Test-Time Augmentation

Test-time augmentation (TTA) is a technique analogous to ensemble learning (i.e. aggregating predictions output by multiple models), but it leverages data augmentation to enable multiple predictions to be made from variants of the same test input by the same model. As such, TTA is more hardware-efficient (i.e. only one trained model is required) than conventional ensemble learning. At inference time, the final prediction was the (ordinary) arithmetic mean of predictions made from the original test input and its augmented variants. The author also experimented with weighted mean using various weighting schemes (e.g. prediction based on original image given more weight, prediction based on horizontal/vertical flip given more weight, etc.), but these were found to yield similar (if not worse) validation performance to the unweighted approach. TTA has been shown to be effective in improving the performance of DL models for skin lesion classification in previous studies [25, 26].

3   Results

As seen in Table 2, the ResNet-18 model achieved a Qk score of 0.910 on the validation set with mix-up augmentation (results without mix-up augmentation are not shown because these were derived from experiments using different/deeper architectures). The Qk score was observed to increase to 0.924 when the model was additionally trained on 250 synthesised images, pointing towards improved model robustness to class imbalance because Qk takes the marginal or expected probability of each target class into account per Eq. (4) above (i.e. it takes imbalanced class distribution into account). The same model yielded a mean validation score (averaged across Qk, macro F1 and MS) of 0.904. This was observed to improve further to 0.914 when TTA was implemented using 10 different data augmentations, applied one at a time to each test input: horizontal flip, vertical flip as well as rotation of $\pm 5°$, $\pm 8°$, $\pm 12°$ and $\pm 15°$. Note that this particular combination of augmentations was chosen because it was empirically observed to give the greatest improvement in validation performance. On the test set, the final (i.e. best) model (trained with mix-up augmentation, 250 synthesised images and TTA) achieved a mean score of 0.848. Using a standard CPU on the CodaLab server, the inference time was 0.64 s with TTA and 0.07 s without TTA per image.

Table 2. Validation performance and test performance (reported using the model with the best validation performance) of ResNet-18. *Mix-up*: mix-up augmentation; *Synthesised*: 250 synthesised training examples included; *TTA*: test-time augmentation; *Qk*: quadratic weighted Cohen's Kappa; *Macro F1*: macro-averaged F1 score; *MS*: macro-averaged specificity.

Score	Validation			Test
	Mix-up	*Mix-up + Synthesised*	*Mix-up + Synthesised + TTA*	
Qk	0.910	0.924	0.927	**0.879**
Macro F1	0.839	0.836	0.861	**0.723**
MS	0.943	0.951	0.953	**0.942**
Mean	*0.897*	*0.904*	*0.914*	*0.848*

4 Conclusions and Future Directions

This work presented a clinically guided approach for training DL models to automatically classify MM from colour fundus photographs. Specifically, a novel image synthesis pipeline was introduced to mitigate class imbalance in the original dataset. This, coupled with the use of mix-up augmentation during training and ensemble prediction via TTA, allowed the final model to accurately differentiate between varying severities of MM. Thus, the model is anticipated to be useful in facilitating population-based screening for MM, particularly in epidemiological research working with large-scale datasets like the UK Biobank [27]. That said, the model's generalisability to populations outside China remains unclear. Besides, the current model is unable to detect the three PM "plus" lesions—lacquer cracks, mCNV and Fuchs spot—on top of MM, as ground-truth labels for these lesions were not available in the MMAC dataset.

Future studies could extend the scope of the present work and frame the problem as a *multilabel* (as opposed to multiclass) classification task—in which MM and the "plus" lesions are treated as non-mutually exclusive labels (i.e. an image can have MM and "plus" lesions concurrently). Alongside enhanced clinical utility, incorporating these "plus" lesions may further improve model performance on account of their strong clinical association with MM. For instance, the majority of macular atrophy is attributable to the development of mCNV [2]. The presence of such (meaningful) correlations between MM and "plus" lesions suggests that an optimal training approach would involve integrating label-specific features with inter-label correlations in one way or another, rather than training multiple binary classifiers independently of one another [28, 29].

To the best of the author's knowledge, this work is the first to demonstrate the benefits of applying image synthesis and domain knowledge to enhance DL performance for MM classification. As such, the contributions of this work lie not solely in the development of a DL model that achieved competitive classification performance, but also in showcasing how clinical domain knowledge can be incorporated into the learning process in innovative ways [30]. While further research is necessary to determine its clinical applicability, thoughtful design and careful implementation of image synthesis could prove beneficial for classification tasks dealing with severe class imbalance. Future work could further explore DL methods such as generative adversarial networks [31] to synthesise potentially more realistic and useful training images for robust PM/MM classification.

References

1. Jonas, J.B., Spaide, R.F., Ostrin, L.A., Logan, N.S., Flitcroft, I., Panda-Jonas, S.: IMI-nonpathological human ocular tissue changes with axial myopia. Invest. Ophthalmol. Vis. Sci. **64**, 5 (2023)
2. Ohno-Matsui, K., et al.: IMI pathologic myopia. Invest. Ophthalmol. Vis. Sci. **62**, 5 (2021)
3. Ohno-Matsui, K., et al.: International photographic classification and grading system for myopic maculopathy. Am. J. Ophthalmol. **159**, 877-883.e877 (2015)
4. Li, J., et al.: Automated detection of myopic maculopathy from color fundus photographs using deep convolutional neural networks. Eye Vis. (Lond) **9**, 13 (2022)

5. Rauf, N., Gilani, S.O., Waris, A.: Automatic detection of pathological myopia using machine learning. Sci. Rep. **11**, 16570 (2021)
6. Hemelings, R., Elen, B., Blaschko, M.B., Jacob, J., Stalmans, I., De Boever, P.: Pathological myopia classification with simultaneous lesion segmentation using deep learning. Comput. Methods Programs Biomed. **199**, 105920 (2021)
7. Cui, J., Zhang, X., Xiong, F., Chen, C.L.: Pathological myopia image recognition strategy based on data augmentation and model fusion. J. Healthc. Eng. **2021**, 5549779 (2021)
8. Tan, T.E., et al.: Retinal photograph-based deep learning algorithms for myopia and a blockchain platform to facilitate artificial intelligence medical research: a retrospective multicohort study. Lancet Digit. Health **3**, e317–e329 (2021)
9. Himami, Z.R., Bustamam, A., Anki, P.: Deep learning in image classification using dense networks and residual networks for pathologic myopia detection. In: 2021 International Conference on Artificial Intelligence and Big Data Analytics, pp. 1–6. (2021)
10. Dai, S., Chen, L., Lei, T., Zhou, C., Wen, Y.: Automatic detection of pathological myopia and high myopia on fundus images. In: 2020 IEEE International Conference on Multimedia and Expo (ICME), pp. 1–6. (2020)
11. Ali, S., Raut, S.: Detection of pathological myopia from fundus images. In: Sharma, H., Shrivastava, V., Bharti, K.K., Wang, L. (eds.) Communication and Intelligent Systems. Lecture Notes in Networks and Systems, vol. 686, pp. 201-208. Springer, Singapore (2023). https://doi.org/10.1007/978-981-99-2100-3_17
12. Park, S.J., Ko, T., Park, C.K., Kim, Y.C., Choi, I.Y.: Deep learning model based on 3D optical coherence tomography images for the automated detection of pathologic myopia. Diagnostics (Basel) **12**, 742 (2022)
13. Lu, L., et al.: Development of deep learning-based detecting systems for pathologic myopia using retinal fundus images. Commun. Biol. **4**, 1225 (2021)
14. Du, R., et al.: Deep learning approach for automated detection of myopic maculopathy and pathologic myopia in fundus images. Ophthalmol. Retina **5**, 1235–1244 (2021)
15. Lu, L., et al.: AI-model for identifying pathologic myopia based on deep learning algorithms of myopic maculopathy classification and "plus" lesion detection in fundus images. Front. Cell Dev. Biol. **9**, 719262 (2021)
16. Tang, J., et al.: An artificial-intelligence-based automated grading and lesions segmentation system for myopic maculopathy based on color fundus photographs. Transl. Vis. Sci. Technol. **11**, 16 (2022)
17. Fang, H., et al.: PALM: open fundus photograph dataset with pathologic myopia recognition and anatomical structure annotation (2023). arXiv:2305.07816
18. Itoi, M., Hieda, O., Kusada, N., Miyatani, T., Kojima, K., Sotozono, C.: Progression of myopic maculopathy: a systematic review and meta-analysis. Eye Contact Lens **49**, 83–87 (2023)
19. Zhang, H., Cisse, M., Dauphin, Y.N., Lopez-Paz, D.: mixup: beyond empirical risk minimization (2017). arXiv:1710.09412
20. Chang, O., Tran, D.N., Koishida, K.: Single-channel speech enhancement using learnable loss mixup. In: Interspeech, pp. 2696–2700 (2021)
21. Czodrowski, P.: Count on kappa. J. Comput. Aided Mol. Des. **28**(11), 1049–1055 (2014). https://doi.org/10.1007/s10822-014-9759-6
22. Cohen, J.: A coefficient of agreement for nominal scales. Educ. Psychol. Measur. **20**, 37–46 (1960)
23. Zhao, X., et al.: Morphological characteristics and visual acuity of highly myopic eyes with different severities of myopic maculopathy. Retina **40**, 461–467 (2020)
24. Szegedy, C., Vanhoucke, V., Ioffe, S., Shlens, J., Wojna, Z.: Rethinking the inception architecture for computer vision (2015). arXiv:1512.00567
25. Perez, F., Vasconcelos, C., Avila, S., Valle, E.: Data augmentation for skin lesion analysis (2018). arXiv:1809.01442

26. Matsunaga, K., Hamada, A., Minagawa, A., Koga, H.: Image classification of melanoma, nevus and seborrheic keratosis by deep neural network ensemble (2017). arXiv:1703.03108
27. Chua, S.Y.L., et al.: Cohort profile: design and methods in the eye and vision consortium of UK Biobank. BMJ Open **9**, e025077 (2019)
28. Wosiak, A., Glinka, K., Zakrzewska, D.: Multi-label classification methods for improving comorbidities identification. Comput. Biol. Med. **100**, 279–288 (2018)
29. Weng, W., Lin, Y., Wu, S., Li, Y., Kang, Y.: Multi-label learning based on label-specific features and local pairwise label correlation. Neurocomputing **273**, 385–394 (2018)
30. Mosqueira-Rey, E., Hernández-Pereira, E., Alonso-Ríos, D., Bobes-Bascarán, J., Fernández-Leal, Á.: Human-in-the-loop machine learning: a state of the art. Artif. Intell. Rev. **56**, 3005–3054 (2023)
31. Wang, Z., et al.: Generative adversarial networks in ophthalmology: what are these and how can they be used? Curr. Opin. Ophthalmol. **32**, 459–467 (2021)

Classification of Myopic Maculopathy Images with Self-supervised Driven Multiple Instance Learning Network

Jiawen Li[1], Jaehyeon Soon[2], Qilai Zhang[1], Qifan Zhang[2],
and Yonghong He[1(✉)]

[1] Shenzhen International Graduate School, Tsinghua University, Shenzhen, China
{lijiawen21,zhangqilai22}@mails.tsinghua.edu.cn, heyh@sz.tsinghua.edu.cn
[2] Department of Computer Science, Harbin Institute of Technology (Shenzhen),
Shenzhen, China
{jaehyeon_soon,21s151127}@stu.hit.edu.cn

Abstract. Myopia is a high-incidence disease that widely exists across various regions. If left unaddressed, it may escalate into high myopia. The leading cause of visual impairment is myopic maculopathy. Currently, certain deep-learning techniques have been employed for the analysis of images depicting myopic maculopathy in fundus photography. These methods are dedicated to assisting physicians in efficient disease diagnosis. In our work, a deep learning framework is introduced to classify images of five different severities of myopic maculopathy. First, we employ a diffusion model to generate a series of images for data augmentation to alleviate the pressure of uneven distribution of categories in training datasets, then we divide images into multiple patches and perform self-supervised learning to generate patch-level feature embeddings. Building upon the above foundation, an aggregator is proposed based on multiple instance learning to achieve image-level classification. We demonstrate the effectiveness of this method in four sufficient experiments with three key evaluation metrics of quadratic-weighted kappa, F1 score, and specificity. Our approach secured the tenth position in the Myopic Maculopathy Analysis Challenge 2023 (MICCAI MMAC 2023).

Keywords: Classification of myopic maculopathy · Multiple instance learning · Self-supervised learning · Generative data augmentation

1 Introduction

Myopia, induced by the progression of various types of myopic macular degeneration, stands as a significant contributor to worldwide visual impairments and blindness [1,3,17,19,27,35]. Depending on the severity, myopic macular degeneration is categorized into five classes: absence of macular lesions, patchy atrophy of the retinal pigment epithelium, diffuse choroidal atrophy, patchy choroidal

---

J. Li, J. Soon and Q. Zhang—Contributed equally.

atrophy, and macular atrophy [29]. Presently, scholars express growing concern over the rising prevalence of high myopia due to its association with serious visual complications [36]. This apprehension stems from the established link between the degree of myopia progression and increased susceptibility to severe myopic macular degeneration.

The prevailing approach for detecting and preventing myopic macular degeneration involves the utilization of fundus photography, allowing for convenient and timely retinal screening. However, this method relies on the manual examination of individual images, posing challenges in terms of meticulousness and specialized knowledge for healthcare professionals. Currently, artificial intelligence has demonstrated exceptional performance in visual tasks within medical image analysis. Leveraging deep learning techniques, it has the capability to predict abnormalities in fundus images, thus assisting in the detection of myopic macular degeneration and diminishing the necessity for manual scrutiny of individual pathological images.

In the present study, we introduce a self-supervised driven multiple instance learning network for the classification of myopic maculopathy images. Specifically, we first propose a generative data augmentation technique based on the diffusion model to mitigate the challenges posed by the uneven distribution of categories within the training dataset. Subsequently, we partition the images into multiple patches, employ a patch-level feature extractor to obtain generalized feature embeddings and integrate these embeddings into an image-level feature representation through an aggregator based on multiple instance learning. Prediction is then carried out using fully connected layers. The feature extractor undergoes weight updates within a self-supervised learning framework. Our approach achieved a tenth-place ranking in the MICCAI MMAC 2023 competition. The source code is accessible at https://github.com/WonderLandxD/MMACmilnet.

2   Related Work

2.1   Deep Learning in Myopic Maculopathy Analysis

Relevant studies are proposed to analyze myopic maculopathy using deep learning techniques. Utilizing popular convolutional neural network frameworks such as ResNet [12], EfficientNet [33], etc., the classification of myopic maculopathy images has demonstrated promising results [7,14,24,34]. Additionally, some research has focused on designing modules to capture detailed image information [32,38]. Furthermore, models based on the Unet architecture have effectively segmented lesion areas [13] and some work utilize multi-task learning to evaluate retinal image quality, retinal lesions, and diabetic retinopathy grades [4,22]. The existing methods do not locate the lesion area or require manual annotation to segment the lesion area. Our method use attention-based MIL to locate the lesion area in weakly supervised manner.

2.2   Multiple Instance Learning

Multiple instance learning (MIL) approaches characterize multiple instances with a singular overarching class label [26]. These methods have found significant application in weakly annotated medical imaging challenges, most notably in the classification of histopathology whole slide images [8]. At present, corresponding work has designed a deep learning network based on a multiple instance learning method to aggregate feature embeddings, such as attention mechanism [18], level clustering [25], and self-attention mechanism [31]. The integration of attention scores enables MIL to be formulated as a learnable neural network that effectively encodes individual instances.

2.3   Self-supervised Learning

Self-supervised learning derives intrinsic supervisory signals from large-scale unlabeled data, utilizing these self-generated supervisory cues to train neural networks. This mechanism enables the extraction of meaningful representations beneficial for subsequent tasks. To date, various self-supervised tasks have been proposed, such as image recolorization [37], transformation prediction [9], image restoration [30], and patch reordering [28]. In essence, self-supervised learning facilitates the preliminary encoding of images through unsupervised signals, optimizing the initialization of feature inputs for downstream applications.

3   Methodology

Our proposed method for macular lesion image classification mainly consists of two parts. The first part is generative data augmentation; the second part is backbone architecture. Our workflow is shown in Fig. 1.

3.1   Generative Data Augmentation

To alleviate the pressure of uneven distribution of categories in training datasets, further expand the number and diversity of training samples, and enhance the generalization ability of the model, we use the diffusion model for generative data augmentation. Specifically, we follow classifier-free guidance [16] to generate additional datasets with class labels. The whole process mainly includes training and sampling.

Suppose the given image x_0 with label y follow distribution $(x_0, y) \sim q(x_0, y)$. The diffusion model defines a Markov chain with total step T that progressively adds noise in the forward process and progressively denoises in the reverse process. At any time t in the forward process, we sample noise from standard normal distribution $\epsilon_t \sim N(0, \mathbf{I})$ and add noise to image $x_t = \sqrt{\alpha_t} x_{t-1} + \sqrt{1 - \alpha_t} \epsilon_t$, where α_t is held constant as hyperparameters. In reverse process, we use model ϵ_θ to denoise image $x_{t-1} = \frac{1}{\sqrt{\alpha_t}}(x_t - \frac{1-\alpha_t}{\sqrt{1-\alpha_t}} \epsilon_\theta(x_t, y, t)) + \sigma_t z$ where σ_t is fixed to constant and $z \sim N(0, \mathbf{I})$.

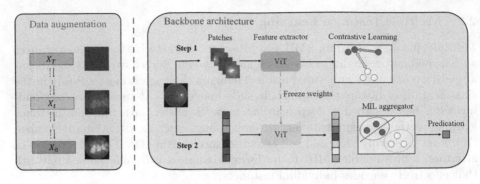

Fig. 1. Our framework for classification of myopic maculopathy images. The diffusion model for data augmentation is used to alleviate the pressure of uneven distribution of categories in training datasets. In the first step, self-supervised DINO is used to train patch-level feature extractors. In the second step, MIL aggregator is used to aggregate patch features to obtain image-level feature representation, and then predict images.

In training steps, we sample $t \sim Uniform(0, T)$ and noise $\epsilon \sim N(0, \mathbf{I})$, and randomly discard conditioning that $y = \emptyset$ with probability p_{uncond} to train unconditionally. We train the model with the loss:

$$L_t = \|\epsilon - \epsilon_\theta(\sqrt{\overline{\alpha}_t}x_0 + \sqrt{1 - \overline{\alpha}_t}\epsilon, y, t)\| \tag{1}$$

where $\overline{\alpha}_t = \prod_{s=1}^{t} \alpha_s$ and the training steps is repeated over times.

In sampling steps, we use the linear combination of the conditional and unconditional score estimates $\widetilde{\epsilon}_t = (1 + \omega)\epsilon_\theta(x_t, y, t) - \omega\epsilon_\theta(x_t, t)$ and recover $x_{t-1} = \frac{1}{\sqrt{\alpha_t}}(x_t - \frac{1-\alpha_t}{\sqrt{1-\overline{\alpha}_t}}\widetilde{\epsilon}_t) + \sigma_t z$ where ω is a conditional scale.

3.2   Backbone Architecture

We now present the backbone architecture. The training component of the Backbone architecture is bifurcated into two phases.

The initial phase is dedicated to training a patch-level feature extractor. We divide each myopic maculopathy image into 16 equitably sized patches (160×160 pixels) and input them into the self-supervised contrastive learning framework, DINO [2]. Specifically, each patch undergoes dual random augmentations and is respectively fed into the teacher and student models. The cross-entropy loss is then computed, utilizing the similarity between the two as the loss function to optimize the model. Both the teacher and student models employ the Vision Transformer model, maintaining identical size. The teacher utilizes the stop-gradient operation to propagate gradients to the student. Parameters of the teacher are updated through exponential moving average. Through self-supervised training via the DINO paradigm, the teacher model acquires the capability to extract efficacious features at the patch level. The process of training patch level feature extractors using DINO is shown in Fig. 2.

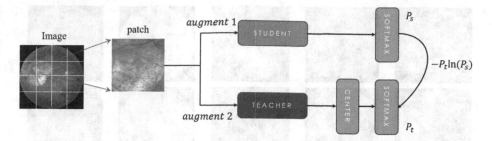

Fig. 2. The process of training patch level feature extractors using DINO.

In the second phase, we focus on training the image-level MIL aggregator. We employ the fixed weights of the teacher model from the initial phase to extract feature embeddings for each patch. Subsequently, these embeddings are integrated into a multiple instance learning framework, underpinned by an attention mechanism [18], to facilitate the training of the MIL aggregator. The attention mechanism is represented as follows:

$$\mathbf{z} = \sum_{k=1}^{K} b_k \mathbf{h}_k \tag{2}$$

where,

$$b_k = \frac{exp\{\mathbf{w}^{\mathrm{T}}\tanh(\mathbf{V}\mathbf{h}_k^{\mathrm{T}})\}}{\sum_{j=1}^{K} exp\{\mathbf{w}^{\mathrm{T}}\tanh(\mathbf{V}\mathbf{h}_j^{\mathrm{T}})\}} \tag{3}$$

where, $\mathbf{h}_k$ is the patch-level feature embedding, $\mathbf{w}$ and $\mathbf{V}$ are learnable parameters. The feature embedding $\mathbf{z}$ of image is obtained by weighting the attention score b_k with the feature embedding of patch. Finally, $\mathbf{z}$ passes through a fully connected layer, and the predicted value of the image can be obtained. The parameters of the attention-based MIL aggregator are updated with cross-entropy loss.

4   Experiments

4.1   Datasets and Implementation

Datasets. We conducted experiments on the data set in Task 1 of Myopic Maculopathy Analysis Challenge 2023. The dataset contains 1143 training images and 248 validation images, which are divided into 5 categories according to the degree of lesions. The evaluation metrics employed include the quadratic weighted kappa, F1 score, and specificity.

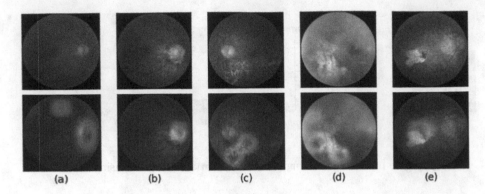

Fig. 3. The first line displays samples of different categories in the validation set. The second line displays the heatmap obtained by visualizing the attention score of MILNet. (a) no macular lesions (b) tessellated fundus (c) diffuse chorioretinal atrophy (d) patchy chorioretinal atrophy (e) macular atrophy

Implementation. In diffusion model, we follow UNet architecture in DDPM [15] and we use a sigmoid variance schedule with timesteps $T = 1000$ for noise schedule. For classifier-free guidance, we set p_{uncond} to 0.5 and ω to 6. In the self-supervised training phase, we use vit-small [6] as the backbone and train it from scratch, epoch size is set to 3000, and other hyperparameters are consistent with DINO [2]. During the training phase of MIL, we select 40 as epoch size, 16 as batch size, 0.0001 as learning rate, Adam [20] as the optimizer with (0.5, 0.9) beta and 0.005 weight. All experiments are done with 4 NVIDIA RTX 3090 GPUs.

4.2   Results

Table 1. Quantitative evaluation results (expressed in %) with different deep learning classification networks. The best result is in **bold**.

Methods	Kappa	F1-score	Specificity	Average
ResNet-50 [12]	74.87	63.26	89.31	75.81
ViT-small [6]	76.80	55.12	87.28	73.07
Swin-T [23]	80.75	60.67	89.72	77.05
HRViT-b1 [10]	71.44	60.47	88.15	73.36
ViG-S [11]	80.42	56.94	91.30	76.22
MILNet (ours)	**86.09**	**75.63**	**94.12**	**85.28**

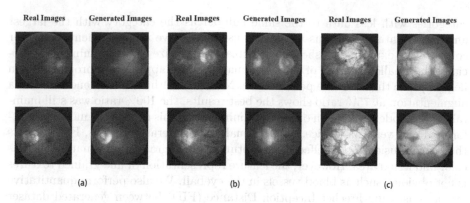

Fig. 4. The first line displays the real images of different categories in the validation set. The second line displays the corresponding images generated by diffusion model. (a) diffuse chorioretinal atrophy (b) patchy chorioretinal atrophy (c) macular atrophy

Comparison with Other Deep Learning Networks. Table 1 delineates a comparative analysis of our method, termed MILNet, against other deep learning networks in the domain of computer vision. Whether considering convolutional neural networks with a residual structure [12], Vision Transformers [6] and their derivatives based on self-attention mechanisms [10,23], or graph convolutional neural networks tailored for visual tasks [11], MILNet consistently manifests superior performance across all evaluation metrics. It is noteworthy that the SwinTransformer [23], rooted in the Transformer architecture, outperforms convolutional neural networks and graph convolutional neural networks of similar parameter magnitude. However, the original Vision Transformer lags behind in comparison to other networks. Heatmaps of representative samples from the validation set are illustrated in Fig. 3.

Table 2. Comparison results of different ratios of generative data augmentation. The best result is in **bold**.

Ratio	Kappa	F1-score	Specificity	Average
0%	88.21	69.29	93.75	83.75
25%	86.64	70.04	94.28	83.65
50%	**88.58**	72.19	94.46	85.08
75%	88.14	**76.61**	**94.71**	**86.49**
100%	86.09	75.63	94.12	85.28

Benefits of Generative Data Augmentation. Table 2 shows the impact on the results of using the diffusion model to expand the data in different proportions. A ratio of 100% means that we have expanded all the remaining four categories with less data to the same number as the category with the largest amount of data. 0% means we do not use generative data augmentation. Our comparative experiments show that increasing the size of the training set, especially the smaller number of category images, in an appropriate proportion can help improve the inference performance. Note that although the generative data augmentation at 75% ratio shows the best results, the 100% ratio was still maintained for model training in our final training, since this ratio is the most straightforward and versatile choice. For the quality of generated images, Fig. 4 shows that our diffusion model effectively captures coarse-grained information such as color and lesion area. However, the feature representation of fine-grained textures is not obvious, such as blood vessels in the eyeball. We also perform quantitative evaluations using Fréchet Inception Distance (FID) between generated dataset and validation dataset and the FID score is 76.74.

Table 3. Comparison results of different pretrained feature extractor. The best result is in **bold**.

Features	Kappa	F1-score	Specificity	Average
Random	49.94	34.58	78.58	54.37
ImageNet [5]	**88.70**	72.31	**94.57**	85.19
DINO [2]	86.09	**75.63**	94.12	**85.28**

Benefits of Self-supervised Learning. Table 3 presents a comparative assessment of different pre-trained feature extractors based on the Vision Transformer model. While DINO does not perform better than ImageNet [5] pretrained models in terms of Kappa and Specificity, it excels in the F1-score, which is an evaluation metric significant for multi-class tasks in datasets with irregular distribution. Therefore, it is more reasonable to utilize a feature extraction mechanism based on DINO pre-training.

Table 4. Comparison results of different MIL aggregators. The best result is in **bold**.

Aggregator	Kappa	F1-score	Specificity	Average
ABMIL [18]	**86.09**	**75.63**	**94.12**	**85.28**
CLAM-MB [25]	83.99	64.97	92.41	80.45
TransMIL [31]	81.96	71.28	91.56	81.60
DSMIL [21]	85.81	66.74	93.51	82.02

Comparison of Different Aggregators. Table 4 presents a comparative analysis of different MIL aggregators. The Aggregator based on the gated attention mechanism (ABMIL) [18] demonstrated superior performance in the classification task for myopic maculopathy images. While several other MIL aggregation strategies outperformed in the context of whole slide image classification [21,25,31], ABMIL exhibited enhanced generalization capabilities when applied to myopic macular images. Consequently, we adopted the ABMIL strategy for designing the feature aggregation module of the network.

5 Conclusion

In this work, a self-supervised driven multiple instance learning network is proposed to solve the classification problem of myopic maculopathy images. We first used a generative data augmentation method to expand images with severe lesions to alleviate the problem of uneven data distribution. Then utilizing the self-supervised learning strategy based on DINO, the Vision Transformer is pretrained to be used as a patch-level feature extractor. Finally, a multiple instance learning aggregator with a gated attention mechanism is designed to aggregate patch-level feature embeddings to obtain image features and achieve prediction after inputting it in a fully connected layer. We demonstrate the effectiveness of this method in four sufficient experiments, including comparing with other visual deep learning networks, the different proportions of generative data augmentation, the benefit of self-supervised strategies, and the comparison of different multiple instance learning aggregators. Our method achieves the 10th best results for task 1, MICCAI MMAC 2023.

Acknowledgements. The work was supported in part by the National Science Foundation of China (NSFC) under Grant 61975089; in part by the grant from the Shenzhen Science and Technology Innovation Commission (Number: KCXFZ20201221173207022, WDZC20202008211141349001, JCYJ20200109110606054). The authors declare that they have no known competing financial interests or personal relationships that could have appeared to influence the work reported in this paper.

References

1. Buch, H., Vinding, T., La Cour, M., Appleyard, M., Jensen, G.B., Nielsen, N.V.: Prevalence and causes of visual impairment and blindness among 9980 scandinavian adults: the Copenhagen City eye study. Ophthalmology **111**(1), 53–61 (2004)
2. Caron, M., et al.: Emerging properties in self-supervised vision transformers. In: Proceedings of the IEEE/CVF International Conference on Computer Vision, pp. 9650–9660 (2021)
3. Cotter, S.A., Varma, R., Ying-Lai, M., Azen, S.P.: Causes of low vision and blindness in adult Latinos
4. Dai, L., et al.: A deep learning system for detecting diabetic retinopathy across the disease spectrum. Nat. Commun. **12**(1), 3242 (2021)

5. Deng, J., Dong, W., Socher, R., Li, L.-J., Li, K., Fei-Fei, L.: ImageNet: a large-scale hierarchical image database. In: 2009 IEEE Conference on Computer Vision and Pattern Recognition, pp. 248–255. IEEE (2009)
6. Dosovitskiy, A., et al.: An image is worth 16x16 words: transformers for image recognition at scale. arXiv preprint arXiv:2010.11929 (2020)
7. Ran, D., et al.: Deep learning approach for automated detection of myopic maculopathy and pathologic myopia in fundus images. Ophthalmol. Retina 5(12), 1235–1244 (2021)
8. Gadermayr, M., Tschuchnig, M.: Multiple instance learning for digital pathology: a review on the state-of-the-art, limitations & future potential. arXiv preprint arXiv:2206.04425 (2022)
9. Gidaris, S., Singh, P., Komodakis, N.: Unsupervised representation learning by predicting image rotations. arXiv preprint arXiv:1803.07728 (2018)
10. Gu, J., et al.: Multi-scale high-resolution vision transformer for semantic segmentation. In: Proceedings of the IEEE/CVF Conference on Computer Vision and Pattern Recognition, pp. 12094–12103 (2022)
11. Han, K., Wang, Y., Guo, J., Tang, Y., Enhua, W.: Vision GNN: an image is worth graph of nodes. Adv. Neural. Inf. Process. Syst. 35, 8291–8303 (2022)
12. He, K., Zhang, X., Ren, S., Sun, J.: Deep residual learning for image recognition. In: Proceedings of the IEEE Conference on Computer Vision and Pattern Recognition, pp. 770–778 (2016)
13. Hemelings, R., Elen, B., Blaschko, M.B., Jacob, J., Stalmans, I., De Boever, P.: Pathological myopia classification with simultaneous lesion segmentation using deep learning. Comput. Methods Programs Biomed. 199, 105920 (2021)
14. Himami, Z.R., Bustamam, A., Anki, P.: Deep learning in image classification using dense networks and residual networks for pathologic myopia detection. In: 2021 International Conference on Artificial Intelligence and Big Data Analytics, pp. 1–6. IEEE (2021)
15. Ho, J., Jain, A., Abbeel, P.: Denoising diffusion probabilistic models. Adv. Neural. Inf. Process. Syst. 33, 6840–6851 (2020)
16. Ho, J., Salimans, T.: Classifier-free diffusion guidance. arXiv preprint arXiv:2207.12598 (2022)
17. Holden, B.A., et al.: Global prevalence of myopia and high myopia and temporal trends from 2000 through 2050. Ophthalmology 123(5), 1036–1042 (2016)
18. Ilse, M., Tomczak, J., Welling, M.: Attention-based deep multiple instance learning. In: International Conference on Machine Learning, pp. 2127–2136. PMLR (2018)
19. Iwase, A., et al.: Prevalence and causes of low vision and blindness in a Japanese adult population: the Tajimi study. Ophthalmology 113(8), 1354–1362 (2006)
20. Kingma, D.P., Ba, J.: Adam: a method for stochastic optimization. arXiv preprint arXiv:1412.6980 (2014)
21. Li, B., Li, Y., Eliceiri, K.W.: Dual-stream multiple instance learning network for whole slide image classification with self-supervised contrastive learning. In: Proceedings of the IEEE/CVF Conference on Computer Vision and Pattern Recognition, pp. 14318–14328 (2021)
22. Liu, R., et al.: DeepDRiD: diabetic retinopathy-grading and image quality estimation challenge. Patterns 3(6), 100512 (2022)
23. Liu, Z., et al.: Swin transformer: hierarchical vision transformer using shifted windows. In: Proceedings of the IEEE/CVF International Conference on Computer Vision, pp. 10012–10022 (2021)

24. Li, L., et al.: AI-model for identifying pathologic myopia based on deep learning algorithms of myopic maculopathy classification and "plus" lesion detection in fundus images. Front. Cell Dev. Biol. **9**, 719262 (2021)
25. Lu, M.Y., et al.: Data-efficient and weakly supervised computational pathology on whole-slide images. Nat. Biomed. Eng. **5**(6), 555–570 (2021)
26. Maron, O., Lozano-Pérez, T., A framework for multiple-instance learning. In: Advances in Neural Information Processing Systems, vol. 10 (1997)
27. Morgan, I.G., Ohno-Matsui, K., Saw, S.-M.: Myopia. The Lancet **379**(9827), 1739–1748 (2012)
28. Noroozi, M., Favaro, P.: Unsupervised learning of visual representations by solving jigsaw puzzles. In: Leibe, B., Matas, J., Sebe, N., Welling, M. (eds.) ECCV 2016. LNCS, vol. 9910, pp. 69–84. Springer, Cham (2016). https://doi.org/10.1007/978-3-319-46466-4_5
29. Ohno-Matsui, K., et al.: International photographic classification and grading system for myopic maculopathy. Am. J. Ophthalmol. **159**(5), 877–883 (2015)
30. Pathak, D., Krahenbuhl, P., Donahue, J., Darrell, T., Efros, A.A.: Context encoders: feature learning by inpainting. In: Proceedings of the IEEE Conference on Computer Vision and Pattern Recognition, pp. 2536–2544 (2016)
31. Shao, Z., et al.: TransMIL: transformer based correlated multiple instance learning for whole slide image classification. Adv. Neural. Inf. Process. Syst. **34**, 2136–2147 (2021)
32. Yun Sun, Yu., et al.: A deep network using coarse clinical prior for myopic maculopathy grading. Comput. Biol. Med. **154**, 106556 (2023)
33. Tan, M., Le, Q.: EfficientNet: rethinking model scaling for convolutional neural networks. In: International Conference on Machine Learning, pp. 6105–6114. PMLR (2019)
34. Wang, R., et al.: Efficacy of a deep learning system for screening myopic maculopathy based on color fundus photographs. Ophthalmol Therapy **12**(1), 469–484 (2023)
35. Xu, L., et al.: Causes of blindness and visual impairment in urban and rural areas in beijing: the beijing eye study. Ophthalmology **113**(7), 1134-e1 (2006)
36. Yokoi, T., Ohno-Matsui, K.: Diagnosis and treatment of myopic maculopathy. Asia-Pac. J. Ophthalmol. **7**(6), 415–421 (2018)
37. Zhang, R., Isola, P., Efros, A.A.: Colorful image colorization. In: Leibe, B., Matas, J., Sebe, N., Welling, M. (eds.) ECCV 2016, Part III. LNCS, vol. 9907, pp. 649–666. Springer, Cham (2016). https://doi.org/10.1007/978-3-319-46487-9_40
38. Zhu, S.-J., et al.: Research on classification method of high myopic maculopathy based on retinal fundus images and optimized alfa-mix active learning algorithm. Int. J. Ophthalmol. **16**(7), 995 (2023)

Self-supervised Learning and Data Diversity Based Prediction of Spherical Equivalent

Di Liu[1,2,3]([✉]), Li Wei[1], and Bo Yang[1]

[1] AIFUTURE Lab, Beijing 100088, China
{weili,yangbo,liudi}@mtwlai.com
[2] National Digital Health Center of China Top Think Tanks, Beijing Normal
University, Beijing 100875, China
[3] School of Journalism and Communication, Beijing Normal University,
Beijing 100875, China

Abstract. This report presents the technical details of the approach of
Team AIfuture for the Myopic Maculopathy Analysis Challenge Task 3.
The approach focuses on the following two aspects: the shift in data distribution between pre-trained and competition datasets, and the diversity of data sample. The ResNet-50 backbone is used to establish a strong
baseline, and the first two-stage blocks are frozen. To alleviate the problem of data distribution shift, publicly available medical data is used for
self-supervised learning, utilizing the well-known DINO algorithm. Various data augmentation techniques are employed to increase the diversity
of data samples. Additionally, it has been observed that using a portion
of the training data can significantly improve performance. Finally, test-
time data augmentation is used for ensemble prediction, which greatly
enhances model performance. The achieved R^2 score of 0.8636 and MAE
score of 0.7326 on the test data result in the final rank of 2.

Keywords: Self-supervised learning · Test-time augmentation · Data
diversity

1 Introduction

Myopia, also known as nearsightedness, is a prevalent oculopathy that affects a
large population worldwide. It is characterized by the abnormal curvature of the
cornea, causing light to focus in front of the retina rather than directly on it,
leading to blurry or distant vision. The consequences of myopia are significant,
including visual impairment, myopic retinal detachment, and macular degeneration. Furthermore, myopia is a leading cause of visual impairment worldwide,
affecting over 500 million people [1]. Despite many efforts to curb the problem, myopia prevalence seems to be on the rise [7]. One reason for the increase
in myopia is the increased use of electronic devices, such as smartphones and
tablets, which can lead to shorter and closer focusing distances [4]. While genetic

© The Author(s), under exclusive license to Springer Nature Switzerland AG 2024
B. Sheng et al. (Eds.): MICCAI 2023, LNCS 14563, pp. 106–112, 2024.
https://doi.org/10.1007/978-3-031-54857-4_10

factors are widely considered to play a significant role in the development of myopia, recent studies have also suggested that lifestyle and environmental factors may have a crucial influence. It is crucial to investigate and understand the various factors involved in myopia development to develop effective interventions and preventive measures [9].

However, the diagnosis of myopic maculopathy remains a challenging task, especially the manual inspection of images by eye examiners, which is a time-consuming and heavily reliant task that requires significant experience in order to accurately diagnose myopic maculopathy. One of the main challenges of diagnosing myopic maculopathy is the lack of specific diagnostic criteria or visual tests that can reliably detect the condition. As a result, ophthalmologists often rely on their clinical judgment and experience to make a diagnosis, which can lead to variations in diagnosis rates and severity of symptoms among examiners. To address this issue, researchers have been developing computer-aided diagnosis (CAD) tools that use machine learning algorithms to analyze retinal images and detect signs of myopic maculopathy. In recent years, deep learning has gained tremendous popularity within the realm of medicine, particularly in the diagnosis of diabetic retinopathy. A variety of deep learning techniques have been employed to analyze retinal fundus images and predict the likelihood of diabetic retinopathy [3,6].

To address this challenge, our solution involves two aspects of innovation: (1) Using self-supervised learning methods, such as DINO, to increase the representation ability of the model. This technique addresses the data distribution problem by pre-training the backbone on natural data (ImageNet) and fine-tuning it on medical data. (2) Using random flip and rotation to increase data diversity, which greatly improves model performance. In addition, using a portion of the data for training can alleviate the overfitting problem, resulting in a 0.04 improvement in performance. The details will be described in Sect. 2. Overall, on the test data of the Myopic Maculopathy Analysis Challenge - spherical equivalent prediction, Our method achieves an R^2 of 0.8636 and a mean absolute error (MAE) of 0.7326 on the test data, resulting in the final rank of 2. We hope that our method can bring valuable insights to the field. The method on github is available at: https://github.com/yeungbo/AIFUTURE4MMAC23.git

2 Our Solution

2.1 Baseline

We utilize the widely-used residual network [5] architecture, specifically ResNet-50, as our backbone for extracting visual representations, as shown in Fig. 1. This enables the model to effectively capture the intricate relationships between visual elements, enabling more accurate and sophisticated representations to be learned. The extracted visual feature is then processed through a three-layer multilayer perceptron (MLP), featuring a hidden dimension of 128 and 32, respectively. This multi-layered processing results in the production of the final output, thereby demonstrating the efficacy of our proposed method in various visual tasks.

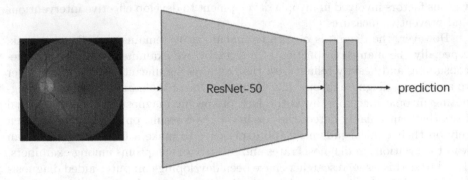

Fig. 1. The framework of our proposed method.

2.2   Self-supervised Learning

First of all, we directly use the pre-trained weights provided by PyTorch, which were pre-trained on the ImageNet-1K dataset, a natural dataset. However, it is observed that there is a problem of data distribution shift between these two datasets. Specifically, the pre-trained weights provided by PyTorch were trained on a dataset of natural images, whereas myopic maculopathy challenge is a medical competition with a significantly different dataset. Another point to consider is that the pre-trained weights provided by PyTorch were trained through a supervised learning paradigm, which is not well-suited for the myopic maculopathy challenge. This is because the supervised learning paradigm assumes a well-defined training set and labels, whereas the myopic maculopathy challenge has a highly unstructured and complex dataset. In recent years, self-supervised learning (SSL) has shown great potential in visual representation learning, where the algorithm learns from the input data without any explicit supervision. This is especially relevant to the myopic maculopathy challenge, as SSL-trained representations are better suited for downstream tasks, as demonstrated by previous research.

Given these considerations, we resort to using the dino algorithm [2], a widely used SSL approach, to perform self-supervised learning on a medical dataset, such as the Rotterdam EyePACS AIROGS train set [8]. This dataset contains over 100,000 color fundus images from 54,274 subjects with a diverse ethnicity, and approximately 500 different sites. Importantly, we do not use the labels contained in this dataset for SSL training, as they may be biased and inaccurate. Instead, we focus on the features learned from the images, which are useful for myopic maculopathy diagnosis and other downstream tasks. In conclusion, we find that self-supervised learning, especially using SSL algorithms, is a promising

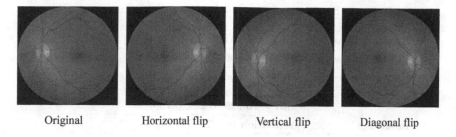

| Original | Horizontal flip | Vertical flip | Diagonal flip |

Fig. 2. Different data augmentation used in test time.

approach for the myopic maculopathy challenge. By leveraging a well-structured and diverse medical dataset, such as the Rotterdam EyePACS AIROGS train set, we can learn high-quality visual representations that are more suitable for downstream tasks, without relying on the biases and inaccuracies of pre-existing labels (Fig. 2).

2.3   Increase Data Diversity

The importance of data diversity in model training cannot be overstated. A lack of diversity in training data can lead to overfitting, where the model becomes too specialized to the training data and is unable to generalize to new data. In the context of computer vision, for example, this may result in the model learning to recognize specific patterns that do not hold true in real-world scenarios.

To mitigate this problem, a variety of data augmentation techniques can be employed to increase the diversity of the training data. This includes techniques such as random horizontal flip, random vertical flip, and random rotation. These techniques help to create new training examples that are similar to the original data but with slight variations, thus exposing the model to a wider range of data and promoting generalization.

In summary, the use of data augmentation techniques is critical in improving the generalization performance of a machine learning model. By increasing the diversity of the training data, these techniques can help to mitigate the risk of overfitting and enable the model to perform well on new, unseen data.

2.4   Part of Data

Another method to prevent overfitting is to reduce the amount of training data. This can prevent the model from memorizing the data and improve its ability to generalize to new instances. To achieve this, we use the train-val-split function from scikit-learn with a validation ratio of 0.2 to obtain 80% training data.

2.5   Test-Time Augmentation

Test-time augmentation (TTA) is a technique widely used in computer vision to enhance the performance of models during inference time. By applying data

Table 1. Summary of the model and training parameters.

External dataset	EyePACS AIROGS train set [8]
Pre-training weights	Dino pre-training with external dataset
Data pre-process	Totensor and Normalization, Norm = (0.485, 0.486, 0.406), Std = (0.229, 0.224, 0.225)
Input-dim	resolution = (720, 720)
Data augmentation	Random-Horizontal-flip, Random-vertical-flip, RandomRotation
Model arch	Resnet50 followed by a three layers of linear projection, whose hidden dim is 128 and 32, respectively
Loss function	Mean square error
optimizer	Adam
Batchsize	64
Learning rate	0.001, decayed at 50-th and 75-th by a factor of 10
Post-process (TTA)	Horizontal-flip, vertical-flip, horizontal-and-vertical flip

augmentation to the test data, TTA generates multiple augmented versions of each test sample. The model then predicts on each augmented sample, and the final prediction is obtained by aggregating the results from all samples. TTA helps to reduce the impact of noise and variability in individual test samples, thereby improving the robustness and generalization of the model. We employ a set of data augmentation techniques, including horizontal and vertical flips and diagonal flips, to perform TTA. These techniques enable us to generate a wide range of augmented versions of the test data, which in turn enables the model to learn and generalize more effectively to new instances.

3   Experiment

3.1   Implement Details

In our experiments, we employ a variant of the Residual Network (ResNet) architecture with 50 layers, commonly referred to as ResNet-50, as our benchmark model. We utilize a batch size of 64 and employ the Adam optimization algorithm in our experimental setup. The learning rate is initially set to 0.001, which is reduced by a factor of 10 at the 50th and 75th epochs, more details can be found in Table 1. The mean square error (MSE) loss function is utilized in our experiments. Our system is deployed on a NVIDIA 2080Ti graphics processing unit (GPU) equipped with 8 GPUs. To initialize the model, we leverage the pre-training procedure using the DINO toolkit on the Rotterdam EyePACS AIROGS training set with the default configuration.

Table 2. Ablation studies on Myopic Maculopathy Analysis Challenge - Task 3. Models are ResNet-50. SSL: Self-supervised learning of DINO on AIROGS data. FL: Freeze the first two Blocks of ResNet-50. HVF: random Horizontal flip and Vertical Flip during training. TTA: Test-Time Augmentation. Rotation: random Rotation during training. Part-data: use Part of data.

SSL	FB	HVF	TTA	Rotation	Part-data	R^2	MAE
						0.6547	1.2030
✓						0.7905	0.9054
✓	✓					0.7912	0.9011
✓	✓	✓				0.8344	0.7930
✓	✓	✓	✓			0.8414	0.7759
✓	✓	✓	✓	✓		0.8432	0.7778
✓	✓	✓	✓	✓	✓	**0.8636**	**0.7326**

3.2 Experiment Results

The experiment results are shown in Table 2. The baseline achieves a R^2 score of 0.6547 and an MAE of 1.2030. To verify the effectiveness of the design, it is consecutively added to the baseline setting. To address the data distribution shift problem, DINO [2] is utilized to pre-train on a publicly available dataset [8], which results in an improvement of 0.1358 for R^2 and 0.2976 for MAE. Furthermore, the ResNet-50 model exhibits overfitting to the training data, which is mitigated by freezing the first two blocks (FB) and further boosting performance. The data diversity of the training data is analyzed, and it is found that most data exhibits a similar pattern, which hinders generalization. To increase data diversity, three data augmentation techniques are applied. HVF significantly boosts performance by achieving an improvement of 0.0432, while Rotation brings an improvement of 0.0018. During the test time, three types of flip strategies are applied to augment the input, and ensemble predictions are generated by fusing their individual predictions. This technique yields an improvement of 0.007 for R^2. Finally, 80% of the training data is used to achieve further improvement.

4 Conclusion

In this challenge, our goal is to optimize the performance of our baseline model by addressing two critical issues: data distribution alignment and data diversity enhancement. We accomplish this by employing a state-of-the-art self-supervised learning method called DINO, which enhances the representation capacity of our model. Additionally, we employ various data augmentation techniques to increase the diversity of the training data, thereby improving the overall performance of our model. To further enhance our model's performance, we implement test-time augmentation, which involves applying transformations to the test data at test time to create new test examples. By leveraging these advanced techniques, we are confident that we can significantly improve the performance of our model on this challenge.

References

1. Abdulhussein, D., Hussein, M.A.: Who vision 2020: have we done it? Ophthalmic Epidemiol. **30**(4), 331–339 (2023). https://doi.org/10.1080/09286586.2022.2127784. pMID: 36178293
2. Caron, M., et al.: Emerging properties in self-supervised vision transformers. In: Proceedings of the IEEE/CVF International Conference on Computer Vision, pp. 9650–9660 (2021)
3. Dai, L., Wu, L.H., et al.: A deep learning system for detecting diabetic retinopathy across the disease spectrum. Nat. Commun. **12**(1), 1–11 (2021)
4. Foreman, J., et al.: Association between digital smart device use and myopia: a systematic review and meta-analysis. Lancet Digit. Health **3**(12), e806–e818 (2021)
5. He, K., Zhang, X., Ren, S., Sun, J.: Deep residual learning for image recognition. In: Proceedings of the IEEE Conference on Computer Vision and Pattern Recognition, pp. 770–778 (2016)
6. Liu, R., Wang, X., Wu, Q., et al.: DeepDRiD: diabetic retinopathy-grading and image quality estimation challenge. Patterns **3**(6), 100512 (2022). https://doi.org/10.1016/j.patter.2022.100512. https://www.sciencedirect.com/science/article/pii/S2666389922001040
7. Resnikoff, S., et al.: Myopia-a 21st century public health issue. Invest. Ophthalmol. Vis. Sci. **60**(3), Mi–Mii (2019)
8. de Vente, C., et al.: AIROGS: artificial intelligence for robust glaucoma screening challenge. arXiv preprint arXiv:2302.01738 (2023)
9. Wang, Y.M., Lu, S.Y., Zhang, X.J., Chen, L.J., Pang, C.P., Yam, J.C.: Myopia genetics and heredity. Children **9**(3), 382 (2022)

Myopic Maculopathy Analysis Using Multi-task Learning and Pseudo Labeling

Hyeonmin Kim[1,2] and Hyeonseob Nam[1(✉)]

[1] Mediwhale, Seoul, South Korea
{luke.kim,alex.nam}@mediwhale.com
[2] Pohang University of Science and Technology (POSTECH), Pohang, South Korea

Abstract. With the advent of deep learning, research has achieved significant success in various fields of ophthalmology, such as diabetic retinopathy detection, glaucoma detection and vessel segmentation. Despite these advancements, there remains a notable gap in the analysis of myopic maculopathy, which carries severe implications such as potential blindness, mainly due to the scarcity of labeled datasets. In addressing this issue, our work in the Myopic Maculopathy Analysis (MMAC) Challenge 2023 focuses on two key tasks. Task 1, Classification of Myopic Maculopathy, aims to accurately categorize the different stages of myopic maculopathy in fundus images. Task 2, Segmentation of Myopic Maculopathy Plus Lesions, requires precisely delineating the areas affected by myopic maculopathy, providing detailed visual maps of the disease's manifestation. We leverage multi-task learning and pseudo-labeling techniques to overcome the challenges posed by the limited availability of labeled data. Through effective integration of these methodologies, we achieve 4th place in Task 1 and 3rd place in Task 2, marking significant strides in the automated analysis of myopic maculopathy.

Keywords: Myopic Maculopathy · Multi-Task Learning · Pseudo Labeling

1 Introduction

Myopic maculopathy [1] refers to degenerative changes in the macula, the central region of the retina, resulting from high myopia or nearsightedness. As the severity of myopia increases, structural changes in the eye, especially the elongation of the eyeball, lead to retinal tissue stretching and thinning. It is clinically categorized by its severity, encompassing conditions such as tessellated fundus, diffuse and patchy chorioretinal atrophy, and macular atrophy. Furthermore, three "Plus" lesions-lacquer cracks, choroidal neovascularization, and Fuchs spot-are recognized as advanced manifestations. Notably, the progression of myopic maculopathy is often rapid following the tessellated fundus stage. Therefore, early diagnosis of myopic maculopathy, facilitated by imaging techniques like fundus photography, is critical to prevent severe visual impairment or blindness. However, study based on deep learning remains limited compared to other popular

© The Author(s), under exclusive license to Springer Nature Switzerland AG 2024
B. Sheng et al. (Eds.): MICCAI 2023, LNCS 14563, pp. 113–119, 2024.
https://doi.org/10.1007/978-3-031-54857-4_11

diseases, e.g. diabetic diseases [2–4]. This emphasizes the ongoing need for extensive research and improved diagnostic tools to manage the vision-threatening aspects of myopic maculopathy.

While the early diagnosis of myopic maculopathy is crucial, the complexity of the disease poses significant challenges for deep learning-based approaches. These methods often require vast amounts of labeled data, which is scarce and costly in this domain. Additionally, the multifaceted nature of the condition necessitates a model capable of handling various tasks, such as differentiating between varying severities and manifestations. These challenges underscore the importance of more advanced approaches than standard supervised learning to effectively utilize the potential of large-scale datasets, including labeled, partially-labeled, and unlabeled data, and to improve diagnostic accuracy and generalization.

In this study, we present an effective yet simple method empowering multitask learning [5] and pseudo-labeling [6], to address the problem of myopic maculopathy diagnosis. It enables us to tackle the multifaceted nature of the disease, as well as harness various partially-labeled or unlabeled datasets. Leveraging the Myopic Maculopathy Analysis (MMAC) Challenge 2023 as our study ground, we focus on two key tasks: Task 1, focusing on the classification of myopic maculopathy, and Task 2, which requires precise segmentation of myopic maculopathy plus lesions. Our results demonstrate the effectiveness of our approach, as we secure the 4th place in Task 1 and the 3rd place in Task 2. These achievements signify notable advancements in the automated analysis of myopic maculopathy and highlight the potential of deep learning techniques in addressing critical challenges in ophthalmology. The source code is made publicly available.[1]

2   Related Work

Multi-task learning [5,7] is a training paradigm that concurrently addresses multiple tasks with a shared model. By jointly learning these tasks, a model can develop richer feature representations and improved generalization capabilities. The benefits of this approach are particularly pronounced when the tasks are closely related and can synergize with each other. With shared representations, the model not only handles various tasks simultaneously but also enhances its performance in solving each task. Additionally, training on multiple tasks serves as a valuable form of self-regularization, effectively preventing overfitting.

Pseudo-labeling [6,8] is a semi-supervised learning approach designed to efficiently utilize unlabeled data. It is particularly valuable in situations where data labeling is expensive or there exists a natural scarcity of labels. Typically, a model is initially trained on a small set of labeled data, after which its predictions on large unlabeled data are generated as pseudo labels. The model is then retrained using both the original labeled data and the pseudo-labeled data. The underlying principle of this approach is that relevant examples tend to be close to each other in the latent space; adapting to a lot of data points with pseudo-labels encourages the model to form smoother decision boundaries. Consequently, it

---

[1] https://github.com/hyeonminkim0625/mmac_multitask.

improves the model's ability to generalize from a limited set of labeled data to a more extensive set of unlabeled data.

Multi-task learning and pseudo-labeling can be effectively combined to complement each other in scenarios where different tasks coexist with label scarcity. Multi-task self-training [9] proposes training independent specialized teacher models for different tasks and subsequently distilling their knowledge into a single generalized student model using pseudo labels generated by the teacher models. In the domain of retinal image analysis, multi-task knowledge distillation [10] focuses on training a model to predict eye disease categories, such as diabetic retinopathy and glaucoma, along with their fine-grained sub-categories and text diagnosis, using teacher models tailored for individual sub-combinations of tasks. To the best of our knowledge, our study is the first to address the problems of myopic maculopathy utilizing multi-task learning and pseudo-labeling, and it shows superior performance without bells and whistles.

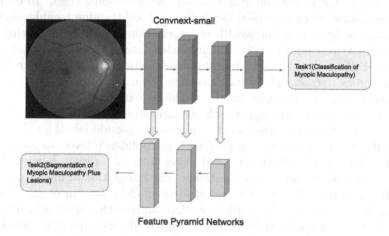

Fig. 1. Our neural network architecture consists of ConvNeXt-small and Feature Pyramid Network. The network is trained for different tasks simultaneously while utilizing pseudo-labels for partially labeled and unlabeled data.

3 Method

We employ a streamlined network architecture which incorporates a ConvNeXt-small [11] backbone along with a Feature Pyramid Network [12] for segmentation, as depicted in Fig. 1. On top of this, we implement multi-task learning and pseudo-labeling strategies, with further details elaborated below.

3.1 Multi-task Learning

We train our model to concurrently address two distinct tasks associated with myopic maculopathy. The first task is classifying fundus images into one of five categories: normal fundus, tessellated fundus, diffuse chorioretinal atrophy, patch chorioretinal atrophy, and macular atrophy, which is defined as Task 1. The second task is the pixel-level segmentation of myopic maculopathy "Plus" lesions with three categories: lacquer cracks (LC), choroidal neovascularization (CNV), and Fuchs spot (FS), which is referred to as Task 2. The integration of these tasks is strategically designed to enable the model to effectively utilize the plus sign as a crucial distinguishing feature, especially in the classification of patch chorioretinal atrophy and macular atrophy. Moreover, this approach is anticipated to aid the model in addressing the data limitations, which are particularly significant in the second task.

3.2   Pseudo-labeling

We face the challenge of limited labeled data in both Task 1 and Task 2, likely due to the rarity of the target conditions as well as the labeling costs. To overcome these constraints, we employ pseudo-labeling and self-training techniques, which are effective in leveraging the wealth of information present in unlabeled data. To this end, we incorporate additional unlabeled datasets, including images from the Palm challenge [14], diabetic retinopathy detection images [13] from Kaggle, and the Airogs dataset [15]. This expansion of our training scope provides a more diverse range of examples for the model to learn from.

Our training paradigm begins with the model being initially trained on the original labeled dataset. Subsequently, we generate pseudo-labels for the various unlabeled datasets, and select those with high confidence levels to ensure label reliability. The model is then retrained using both the original labeled dataset and the additional pseudo-labeled datasets. The integration of multi-task learning, utilized in both the teacher and student models, facilitates simultaneous learning across both tasks. Notably, we adopt an iterative approach, retraining the model three times using the updated high-confidence pseudo-labeled data. Each iteration alternately refines the model and pseudo labels, progressively enhancing the model's accuracy and generalization.

4   Results

We split the datasets for both tasks in an 8:2 ratio, with 80% used for training and 20% for internal validation. The test set is accessible only through the online submission platform, ensuring an unbiased evaluation of our model's performance. We carefully select and tune various hyperparameters to optimize performance on the validation sets. The specific hyperparameters used in our study are detailed in Table 1. We utilize the PyTorch framework for the implementation.

For Task 1, the classification of myopic maculopathy, our model demonstrates remarkable performance on the internal validation set, achieving a Quadratic Weighted Kappa (QWK) of 0.9213, a Macro F1 score of 0.8536, and a Macro

Specificity of 0.9510. On the external test set, the model maintains strong performance with scores of 0.8928 for QWK, 0.7528 for Macro F1, and 0.9409 for Macro Specificity. These results not only highlight the model's accuracy in classifying various stages of myopic maculopathy but also its robustness in generalization. The results for Task 1 are summarized in Table 2.

In Task 2, involving the pixel-level segmentation of myopic maculopathy plus lesions, our model achieves Dice Similarity Coefficients (DSC) of 0.770 for lacquer cracks (LC), 0.7535 for choroidal neovascularization (CNV), and 0.8344 for Fuchs spot (FS) on the internal validation set. For the external test set, the scores are 0.6865 for LC DSC, 0.6490 for CNV DSC, and 0.8317 for FS DSC. These results underscore our model's capability in precise segmentation tasks, a critical aspect in the detailed visualization of the disease. The quantitative results for Task 2 are presented in Table 3, and qualitative examples of the segmentation are illustrated in Fig. 2.

Table 1. Hyperparameters for Task 1 and Task 2.

	Task 1	Task 2
Preprocessing	flip, rotate, crop, blur, equalize, color jitter, and coarse dropout	flip, rotate, crop, blur, equalize, color jitter, and coarse dropout
Model	Convnext-small	Convnext-small
Loss	CrossEntropyLoss	CrossEntropyLoss and DiceLoss
Optimizer	AdamW	AdamW
Ensemble	3 models	3 models
TTA	multi-scaling and flip	multi-scaling and flip
PostProcessing	None	Gaussian Blur

Table 2. Evaluation results for Task 1.

	QWK	Macro F1	Macro Specificity
Validation	0.9213	0.8536	0.9510
Test	0.8928	0.7528	0.9409

Table 3. Evaluation results for Task 2.

	LC DSC	CNV DSC	FS DSC
Validation	0.770	0.7535	0.8344
Test	0.6865	0.6490	0.8317

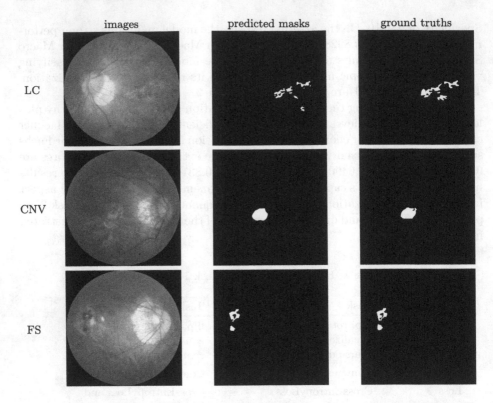

Fig. 2. Visualization of the segmentation results for myopic maculopathy plus lesions.

5   Conclusion

In this paper, we demonstrated a practical approach that leverages the combined strengths of multi-task learning and pseudo-labeling to effectively address the challenges associated with the diagnosis of myopic maculopathy. Our methodology underwent rigorous evaluation in the MMAC challenge, securing high-ranking positions in multiple tasks. These results not only validate the effectiveness of our approach but also serve as a testament to its potential for enhancing diagnostic accuracy in the field of ophthalmology. By successfully addressing the challenges of data scarcity and the complexity of the disease without particularly tailored algorithms, our work lays the groundwork for the development of more scalable and robust diagnostic tools. Future work will focus on expanding its scope to include other ophthalmic conditions, with the aim of further generalizing the applicability of our method.

References

1. Yokoi, T., Ohno-Matsui, K.: Diagnosis and treatment of myopic maculopathy. Asia-Pac. J. Ophthalmol. **7**(6), 415–421 (2018)
2. Dai, L., et al.: A deep learning system for detecting diabetic retinopathy across the disease spectrum. Nat. Commun. **12**(1), 1–11 (2021)
3. Liu, R., et al.: DeepDRiD: diabetic retinopathy-grading and image quality estimation challenge. Patterns **3**, 100512 (2022)
4. Guan, Z., et al.: Artificial intelligence in diabetes management: advancements, opportunities, and challenges. Cell Rep. Med. **4**, 101213 (2023)
5. Nam, H., Han, B.: Learning multi-domain convolutional neural networks for visual tracking. In: Proceedings of the IEEE Conference on Computer Vision and Pattern Recognition (CVPR) (2016)
6. Pham, H., Dai, Z., Xie, Q., Le, Q.V.: Meta pseudo labels. In: Proceedings of the IEEE Conference on Computer Vision and Pattern Recognition (CVPR) (2021)
7. Raffel, C., et al.: Exploring the limits of transfer learning with a unified text-to-text transformer. J. Mach. Learn. Res. **21**(1), 5485–5551 (2020)
8. Xie, Q., Luong, M.-T., Hovy, E., Le, Q.V.: Self-training with noisy student improves imagenet classification. In: Proceedings of the IEEE Conference on Computer Vision and Pattern Recognition (CVPR) (2020)
9. Ghiasi, G., Zoph, B., Cubuk, E.D., Le, Q.V., Lin, T.-Y.: Multi-task self-training for learning general representations. In: Proceedings of the IEEE/CVF International Conference on Computer Vision (ICCV) (2021)
10. Chelaramani, S., Gupta, M., Agarwal, V., Gupta, P., Habash, R.: Multi-task knowledge distillation for eye disease prediction. In: Proceedings of the IEEE/CVF Winter Conference on Applications of Computer Vision (2021)
11. Liu, Z., et al.: A convnet for the 2020s. In: Proceedings of the IEEE Conference on Computer Vision and Pattern Recognition (CVPR) (2022)
12. Lin, T.-Y., Dollár, P., Girshick, R., He, K., Hariharan, B., Belongie, S.: Feature pyramid networks for object detection. In: Proceedings of the IEEE Conference on Computer Vision and Pattern Recognition (CVPR) (2017)
13. Emma Dugas, J., Jorge, W.: Diabetic Retinopathy Detection (2015). https://www.kaggle.com/c/diabetic-retinopathy-detection/
14. Fu, H., et al.: PAthoLogic Myopia Challenge. IEEE Dataport, PALM (2019)
15. De Vente, C., Vermeer, K.A., Jaccard, N., et al.: AIROGS: artificial Intelligence for robust glaucoma screening challenge. IEEE Trans. Med. Imaging **43**, 542–557 (2023)

Author Index

C
Chen, Xiwen   56, 66
Conze, Pierre-Henri   1

D
Ding, Ye   18
Dumitrascu, Oana M.   56

E
El Habib Daho, Mostafa   1

F
Feng, Rui   31, 46

H
He, Yonghong   95
Heras, Jónathan   75
Hou, Junlin   31, 46

J
Jiang, Weili   1
Jin, Panji   18

K
Kim, Hyeonmin   113

L
Lamard, Mathieu   1
Lepore, Natasha   56
Li, Huayu   56, 66
Li, Jiawen   95
Li, Yihao   1
Liu, Di   106
Lu, Li   18

N
Nam, Hyeonseob   113

P
Pan, Xuhao   18

Q
Qiu, Peijie   56
Quellec, Gwenolé   1

S
Soon, Jaehyeon   95

T
Tan, Yubo   1

W
Wang, Hao   56
Wang, Yalin   56, 66
Wang, Zhihan   1
Wei, Li   106

X
Xiao, Fan   31, 46
Xu, Jilan   31, 46
Xu, Yiqian   31, 46

Y
Yang, Bo   106
Yii, Fabian   83

Z
Zhang, Bo   31, 46
Zhang, Jing   1
Zhang, Philippe   1
Zhang, Qifan   95
Zhang, Qilai   95
Zhang, Yuejie   31, 46
Zhu, Wenhui   56, 66
Zou, Haidong   31, 46

B. Sheng et al. (Eds.): MICCAI 2023, LNCS 14563, p. 121, 2024.
https://doi.org/10.1007/978-3-031-54857-4

Printed in the United States
by Baker & Taylor Publisher Services

Printed in the United States
by Baker & Taylor Publisher Services